# Developing the Gifted and Talented Young Learner

# Developing the Gifted and Talented Young Learner

Margaret Sutherland

Los Angeles • London • New Delhi • Singapore • Washington DC

SAGE Publications Ltd
1 Oliver's Yard
55 City Road
London EC1Y 1SP

SAGE Publications Inc.
2455 Teller Road
Thousand Oaks, California 91320

SAGE Publications India Pvt Ltd
B 1/I 1 Mohan Cooperative Industrial Area
Mathura Road
New Delhi 110 044

SAGE Publications Asia-Pacific Pte Ltd
33 Pekin Street #02-01
Far East Square
Singapore 048763

**Library of Congress Control Number: 2007941788**

**British Library Cataloguing in Publication data**

A catalogue record for this book is available from the British Library

ISBN 978-1-4129-4631-5
ISBN 978-1-4129-4632-2 (pbk)

Typeset by C&M Digitals (P) Ltd., Chennai, India
Printed in Great Britain the Cromwell Press, Trowbridge, Wiltshire
Printed on paper from sustainable resources

*For Stacey, Amy and the 'North Lanarkshire girls'. Now you are all qualified teachers make sure you help your children reach for the stars.*

*This book is also dedicated to the memory of Emily-Jane Gold. A gifted and talented young girl. Ready to shine.*

# Contents

# Acknowledgements

My thanks go to the many inspirational 3–5-year-olds I have come across in early years settings.

Thanks go to Stacey Hutton, Amy Cullen and Fiona Huggan for their constructive feedback and to Isobel Reid and Ian Pieper for sharing their experiences. Thanks also to Susan May, Nursery Teacher, Killermont Primary School Nursery Class and the staff of Renfrewshire early years settings for feedback and allowing me to try out ideas.

Special thanks to Shona Mathieson, close friend and Depute Head Teacher of Killermont Primary School, Bearsden, and to Ewan Tooth for technical advice.

Advice and support were gratefully received from my colleagues and friends, Chris Smith, Niamh Stack, Rae Galbraith and Frances Gaughan, and from Jude Bowen and Amy Jarrold at SAGE Publications.

Finally, my thanks go to Andrew and Briagh for 'putting up with me' and constantly encouraging me during the writing process.

# About the author

 Margaret Sutherland lectures at the University of Glasgow in additional support needs. She is also the project leader for the Scottish Network for Able Pupils. She has 26 years' teaching experience in mainstream primary schools, behaviour support and latterly in higher education

She has written articles in the field of gifted and talented education and is author of *Gifted and Talented in the Early Years: A Practical Guide for 3–5 Year Olds.*

She is on the editorial board of the Korean Educational Development Institute, *Journal of Educational Policy.* She speaks regularly at conferences and has led courses, workshops and seminars across the UK and in Korea.

# How to use this book

Early years national initiatives in the United Kingdom (UK) have helped to raise expectations among educators. This, coupled with the move towards inclusive education, has seen many exciting projects taking place in settings across the country. A central issue in the early years has been early identification of the additional support needs of young children. Much of the writing related to this centres on children who 'can't do' certain things. This book, however, is concerned with the children who are doing things beyond what we might expect for their ageIt considers how we can meet their additional needs within an inclusive framework.

Early educational experiences can have a long-lasting effect on us. Most people can recount positive and negative learning experiences. When you ask a bit more about these experiences, people often talk about a particular adult. Where the experience has been positive, they speak highly of the individual and the effect on their learning. Sadly, some recount negative experiences and do so with great feeling. An ill-thought word or a look can have a devastating effect on a child. Sometimes this effect lasts into adulthood. The kind of interaction we engage in with all of the young people in our care is of vital importance. This book considers gifted and talented children and encourages us to explore our beliefs and practice relating to these young learners. By considering this group of children, we will be in a better position to meet the needs of all children in our setting.

The first chapter of this book sets out to consider how young children develop their beliefs about ability. Particular issues for gifted and talented young children and their families, such as sibling rivalry and lack of understanding from relatives, are touched on. Issues for staff working with these children and issues for their age peers are also explored. The reader is asked to think about their own learner identity.

Chapter 2 takes practitioners through a process that leads to them considering how their beliefs about their own ability impact on what they do and say, to and with, young children. Case studies are used to demonstrate the impact of attitudes and beliefs on the young learner and on the tasks they provide.

Chapter 3 explores how staff, parents and young children view the world and how these, sometimes conflicting, narratives can lead to difficulties when challenging and supporting gifted young learners

Chapter 4 considers the various aspects involved in creating and developing challenging, open-ended activities for gifted young children so that they develop a sense of themselves as a learner. It builds on the ideas in previous chapters and, using a story as a starting point, offers some ideas for 'getting started'. The chapter refers to fact sheets for adults and a useful glossary that can be found at the end of the book.

Chapter 5 offers a range of challenging activities related to stars, the sun and space exploration that can be used or adapted for use within the setting.

Chapter 6 examines the idea of identifying through provision. This holistic and inclusive approach allows for latent, potential and unexpected abilities to be identified.

Chapter 7 looks at the kind of feedback we can offer that will help to develop a positive learner identity and effective learning dispositions. It also considers how practitioners can work together with parents.

The final chapter pulls together the thoughts from throughout the book. It explores some of the reasons why it is so difficult to meet the needs of all within the setting. It highlights the need to challenge our gifted and talented children and to ensure that we help to develop positive learner identities in each child with whom we work.

You will see icons appearing throughout this book:

| **Key for Icons** | | | |
|---|---|---|---|
| | | Further reading | 📖 |
| Activity | ▦ | | |
| | | Photocopiable pages | 📄 |
| Case study | 📁 | | |
| | | Points to remember | |
| Chapter objective | ☀🖱 | | |
| | | Summary boxes | ▪ |
| Cross reference | → | | |
| | | To think about | ☁ |

It should be noted that four countries make up the UK. Each has adopted slightly different terminology, and approaches, to the education of gifted and talented learners.

Scotland:            more able pupils.

Northern Ireland:  gifted and talented pupils.

Wales:               more able and talented pupils.

England:             gifted and talented pupils.

While terminology is important, at the heart of each country's approach is the desire to offer every child a relevant, challenging and meaningful learning experience. Placing children at the heart of learning will help us to achieve this.

# 1

# Developing young learners' identity

Some key points about developing young gifted and talented learners' identity are made in this chapter.

> **As early years educators we:**
>
> - **can impact learner identities**
> - **can create positive learning environments**
> - **have a view about our own learner identity**
> - **need to foster positive learning dispositions.**
>
> **We need to remember that:**
>
> - **learner identities can change depending on the learning context**
> - **children who are gifted and talented face issues and have additional support needs?**

## Introduction

The children we care for will be busy developing their identities. It is an exciting time as they work out who they are, what they can do, how they fit into different groups and how they relate to the world about them. Many of the books about identity are concerned with developing social competence. While this is important it is not the focus for this book. This book is about how we, as practitioners, can develop and contribute to a child's 'learner' identity. In other words, how can we help children achieve a greater understanding and acceptance of their own abilities and the abilities of others?

Like all children, those who are gifted and talented will develop learner identities through interaction with others. The experiences they encounter as they are growing up will accumulate and feed into their beliefs about themselves as learners.

Sometimes gifted and talented children assume everyone is the same as them and it is not until they arrive in nursery or school that they realize they have particular abilities. As a gifted child said: 'I thought everybody was the same as me until I went to school.'

The realization that they are in some way different can start early in life. It is important, therefore, that we consider how we act with and react to children in our care who are somehow 'different', since this can have a huge impact on the child's learner identity. Depending on our reaction, we can either leave them with the feeling it is a bad thing to be different, or with the feeling that difference is something positive. Indeed, if a child is relatively unaware of difference until they arrive in an educational setting, we perhaps have to question what our educational settings are doing to exacerbate that difference.

## A good label to have?

If you had to be assigned a label, then you might think that the label of 'gifted and talented' would be a good one to have. After all, being gifted and talented means that you must be really good at something, it might even mean you are really good at everything you try. However, talking to children who have this label, and talking to their parents, challenges this idea. In fact, like any other label, 'gifted and talented' can be problematic for children, peers, parents and educators alike.

## Issues for gifted and talented children

Gifted and talented children can experience:

- jealousy from age peers

- sibling rivalry

- constant pressure to succeed

- being misunderstood by those around them

- an expectation that they will be perfect

- difficulties in forming relationships with peers.

Gifted and talented children tend to process large amounts of information rapidly. When, as is often the case, learning is broken down into small manageable steps, so that all children can understand, the gifted and talented child may become frustrated or even stressed. For such children, complexity and challenge are important and when these are absent from the learning experience they may simply opt out or learn to underachieve. Gifted and talented children can also experience internal conflict as they try to understand and come to terms with their abilities. Unconsciously we may exacerbate the issues faced by young gifted and talented children if, for example, we ignore their abilities.

## Issues for peers

Peers can experience:

- a feeling that they are not as 'good' as the gifted and talented child

- an inability to relate to the gifted and talented child

- being compared to the gifted and talented child

- frustration at not being able to do things the gifted and talented child can do.

Unconsciously we may exacerbate the issues faced by the peers of young gifted and talented children. If we constantly praise the gifted and talented child for what they can do or have achieved, then their peers will feel inadequate. If young children are making sense of the world around them and if they are working out what makes them good or bad, then there is a danger they will believe that their inability to do the things the gifted child can makes them bad (Dweck, 1995).

## Issues for parents

Parents experience:

- jealousy from other parents

- dealing with sibling rivalry

- difficulty helping friends and family to understand their child's abilities

- being misunderstood by those around them

- being classed as a 'pushy parent'

- being worried about finding an educational establishment that will offer an appropriate level of challenge

- wanting their child to find a friend

- trying to understand their child's thought processes

- feeling overwhelmed by the responsibility they have towards their child.

Every parent wants the best for their child, and ultimately this is what we also strive for. The difference is that as educators we are trying to do the best for a large number of children, whereas a parent may be striving to meet the needs of a (hopefully) much smaller number. I have found that many parents of young gifted and talented learners I talk to are trying hard to come to terms with the fact that their young child is so advanced in their learning for their age. They say things like

- I don't know where he/she gets this from. Neither of us are good at maths.

- Her big brother isn't like this.

- I just wish he/she was normal.

- He/she constantly asks questions I don't know the answers to.

They also struggle to reconcile this advancement with the range of age behaviours they demonstrate. When asked to put their toys away they may behave like any other 3-year-old and yet when reading they are like an 8-year-old, and when thinking about global warming they may be more akin to a 22-year-old. These discrepancies can be difficult for all concerned: parents, peers, early years educators and the child.

## Issues for educators

Early years educators experience:

- lack of training in how to support a gifted and talented child

- worrying about how they can cater for the child's needs when they have other children with additional support needs in the group

- disquiet that the child already knows more than they do about specific topics

- concern that the child will develop socially and emotionally as well as academically

- anxiety over the child reaching a plateau in their learning.

We are all keen to do the best for all children in our care, but considering in detail the needs of gifted and talented children does not mean we are excluding others. Meeting the needs of gifted and talented children will help us to meet the needs of all children. Knowing where to go for support and information will also help us to feel we are not alone as we try to cater for individual children in our care. Sometimes we ignore the abilities of young gifted and talented children because we are not sure how best to help and support them.

The label gifted and talented, in and of itself, is neither good nor bad. It is how we react to that label, what we believe about that label and how we offer support to all those involved that will result in the label having a positive or negative effect on a child's view of themselves as a learner.

## Learner identity

We have all developed an identity. Indeed, we may have several identities that change depending on the situation we find ourselves in. These identities will have developed over time and will be the result of many thousands of interactions with friends, family and significant others in our lives. Our learner identity will have been developed and honed according to life experiences and interactions with others during learning experiences. For some children growing up will be confusing and complex due to the circumstances in which they find themselves. As educators we need to consider how this will impact on individual children and how we can best support them. Individual experiences will not necessarily have a long-lasting effect on learner identity, however, we need to be aware that when children experience repeated and consistent activities and reactions to those activities, it will impact on their beliefs about themselves as learners.

 ## Activity

Think about your perception of yourself as a learner. Does it change depending on the circumstances you find yourself in?
Think about the following situations.
How would you approach them?
What effect does it have on you as a learner?

### Scenario 1

You have been responsible for developing learning plans in your setting. They have been used as exemplars by your local education authority. You are asked to work alongside a newly qualified practitioner to further develop the learning plans.

*How do you approach this situation?*

In this situation you may approach the task confidently. After all you know that your work on planning is valued since it has been shared with colleagues. Having more experience than the person you are working with might also contribute to your feeling of confidence.

*What effect does it have on you as a learner?*

In this situation, you might be keen to develop the knowledge you have. Since you already have a good grasp of what learning plans are about you might seek out new knowledge in order to work together with your colleague to develop the plans.

### Scenario 2

You are attending a continuing professional development course. The course leader, who is a well-known figure in early years education, hands out a complex article full of 'jargon' and theoretical standpoints for the group to read and discuss. You have to contribute to the small group and then report back to the larger group.

*How do you approach this situation?*

You might be concerned that you will not understand the complex language used within the article. You could decide to sit quietly and listen to what others say so you have something to report back.

*What effect does it have on you as a learner?*

If the course leader is well known in early years education you may not want to ask for help as this may make you look as though you are not very clever. In addition, you may not want to admit to being unsure of something since you are part of a group. This may also indicate to colleagues that you do not know what the article is about. The result is you might decide to quietly disengage from the learning process.

### Scenario 3

You are attending a jazzercise class for the first time. The very enthusiastic leader splits you into groups. You are nominated to be the leader. You have to learn a sequence of three steps and teach it to the rest of the group. The group will then perform it for the whole class.

*How do you approach this situation?*

You are concerned you will not remember the dance sequence and steps. Even if you do, you are worried that you might not teach them accurately. You are not comfortable with being the focal point within the group.

*What effect does it have on you as a learner?*

Because you are anxious and lacking self-confidence your concentration lapses and you are unable to retain the dance steps. You are reluctant to attend the class again, perceiving to have made a fool of yourself. You are sure someone else in the group would have been a better leader.

### Scenario 4

You are attending an evening class. You have some experience and so sign up for an intermediate course. When you get there, you discover you have much more experience than the others. The tutor does not realize this and so you spend much of your time helping others and not advancing your own skills.

*How do you approach this situation?*

At first you feel confident and are happy to consolidate existing skills and support others who are struggling. As the weeks progress you become frustrated because you have not learned anything new and so you disengage from the class and occasionally miss a week.

*What effect does it have on you as a learner?*

At first you feel confident and are happy to share your knowledge. As the weeks progress and having learned nothing new, you begin to question why you are attending the class. You are disappointed that the tutor has not recognized your abilities and catered for them accordingly. Because it is not meeting your needs or expectations, you reprioritize your time and consequently are not concerned when you the miss the occasional class. Indeed you may even stop attending altogether.

Now consider:

- Does your view of yourself as a person and as a learner change depending on the situation?
- When does it change positively? When does it change negatively?

Of particular interest here is the effect this ability to behave differently has on our learning. In scenario 1, we might feel empowered and are happy to engage in the learning process, working alongside others. In scenario 2, we might simply 'opt out', leaving others to complete the task in order to 'save face'. In scenario 3, our levels of anxiety are such that we cannot 'learn well'. You compare yourself to others and, even without concrete evidence, you decide you are not as good as them and so you consider not returning to the class. Scenario 4 leaves you frustrated with a sense of not learning anything. Of interest here is the fact that this can lead us to reprioritize, with the unchallenging learning experience coming way down our list.

We all behave differently in different situations, and so do children – just think of a time when a parent has told you a child can do something at home that they cannot do in the setting – it may be that the different setting makes all the difference to them!

Already we can see that we can change our identity depending on such things as circumstances, perception, peer reaction, challenge and confidence. At no time have we called into question our ability to complete the tasks, rather it is outside influences that have led us to think we either 'can do this' or 'we cannot do this'.

We can see this in the early years setting. Where children feel valued and where their skills and abilities are acknowledged they will more readily participate in activities. If children feel they cannot do something or if they try and get it wrong – where wrong equals bad – then they may feel disempowered and prefer to melt quietly into the background. Equally, when they get something right and that is not acknowledged or they are 'put down' in order to keep them in their place they simply learn to keep quiet.

## Thinking about learning situations

When we start to analyse learning situations, we can discover two factors: those that help us learn and those that hamper our learning. Think of a time when you had to learn something. It may be from your school days or it could be as an adult. Write down what helped you to learn and what made learning difficult.

Table 1.1 was compiled from work carried out with early years educators, teachers of primary and secondary pupils and student teachers. Compare your ideas with theirs.

**Table 1.1   Factors that help us learn/factors that hamper our learning**

| Factors that help us learn | Factors that hamper our learning |
| --- | --- |
| A desire to learn | No interest in the topic |
| A purpose to the learning | No sense of purpose |
| Enjoying learning | Being talked at for a long time |
| An enthusiastic teacher/coach | Frightened of failure and I will look 'stupid' |
| Being involved in the learning | The teacher not passionate about the subject |
| A teacher/coach who explains things when I don't understand | No one to help me when I'm stuck |
| A pleasant, non-threatening environment | An uncomfortable environment |
| Linking new learning to knowledge I already have | Being worried about other things/have other commitments |
| Having time to learn | Not enough time |
| Feeling secure, satisfied and happy | Feeling tired, hungry, too cold/hot |

Thinking about our own learning offers us vital opportunities to examine our work with children, our interactions, the kind of opportunities we offer children and the kind of support we provide.

Our beliefs about ourselves as learners will help us to better understand our approaches to and interactions with children. As we plan learning activities we need to consider how the learning situation impacts on children's beliefs about their abilities and their learner identity. Lillian Katz (1993) identified four goals for learning:

1. Knowledge.

2. Skills.

3. Dispositions.

4. Feelings.

Typically, education has been more concerned with knowledge and skills than with dispositions and feelings. However, dispositions and feelings would appear to have an important role to play in learning. A child may have the prerequisite skills and knowledge for mathematics but not have a disposition to 'do mathematics'. A child who recognizes numbers to 20, is able to add and subtract and is curious about pattern may, however, be in the process of developing a positive disposition towards mathematics. As such we have to ensure that we foster and develop successful learning dispositions. These dispositions are inextricably linked to our view of ourselves and to our beliefs about what we can and cannot achieve. In other words, these dispositions feed in to our identity as a learner.

## Building a profile of learner identity

Think about the children in your setting. Which words best describe them as a learner?

- Confident.

- Insecure.

- Engaged.

- Disengaged.

Think about the child in different learning contexts. Do the same words still apply? It can be helpful to collate this type of information, as it will help you develop a profile of the child's learner identity and will allow you to see where you need to develop and/or support their positive development. Such dispositions can be incorporated into existing observation formats.

Figure 1.1 will help you to organize this information. It will also allow you to record your evidence for making such decisions about learner identity.

**Cross reference**

This page gives an example of a completed sheet for a child called Kim. A photocopiable sheet is available on page 10. Two blank columns are available so you can add your own descriptions of learners.

**Figure 1.1**   Kim Deacon observation sheet

Name of child: Kim Deacon

Age at next birthday: 5

Date of observation: 10 October 2007

| Activity | Confident | Insecure | Engaged | Disengaged | | |
|---|---|---|---|---|---|---|
| Sand | X | | X | | | |
| Water | X | | X | | | |
| Small world | | | | | | |
| Mark-making | X | | X | | | |
| Large construction | X | | X | | | |
| Games and puzzles | | | | | | |
| Painting | | X | | X | | |
| Role play | | X | | X | | |
| Problem-solving | X | X | X | X | | |

**Evidence**

| Activity | Evidence |
|---|---|
| Sand | Displays knowledge of the properties of sand, i.e. wet, dry etc. is keen to talk about how sand is made. |
| Water | A good knowledge of volume. |
| Small world | N/A for this observation. |
| Mark-making | Interestingly, although Kim doesn't like to paint she is very happy to experiment with mark-making in real-life contexts, e.g. in the café/shop. |
| Large construction | Excellent fine and gross motor skills allow Kim to create complex models. She uses materials in unusual ways and does not stick to convention in terms of building. |
| Games and puzzles | N/A for this observation. |
| Painting | Has to be encouraged to paint. Dislikes getting paint on hands. Spends little time painting before moving on to the next task. |
| Role play | Very reluctant to join in. Does not volunteer ideas or suggestions for tasks but prefers to sit at the back quietly. |
| Problem-solving | Very confident and engaged when the activity is related to construction – can spend a significant amount of time on a task. Kim shows no interest when problem-solving is related to art activities or mathematics. |

If we collect information from a range of activities we can begin to build up Kim's profile so we can identify areas of strength and confidence as well as development needs. Building up this kind of information is useful if we use it to inform our interactions with the children.

**Name of child:**

**Age at next birthday:**

**Date of observation:**

| Activity | Confident | Insecure | Engaged | Disengaged | | |
|---|---|---|---|---|---|---|
| Sand | | | | | | |
| Water | | | | | | |
| Small world | | | | | | |
| Mark-making | | | | | | |
| Large construction | | | | | | |
| Games and puzzles | | | | | | |
| Painting | | | | | | |
| Role play | | | | | | |
| Problem-solving | | | | | | |

**Evidence**

| Activity | Evidence |
|---|---|
| Sand | |
| Water | |
| Small world | |
| Mark-making | |
| Large construction | |
| Games and puzzles | |
| Painting | |
| Role play | |
| Problem-solving | |

As human beings we all respond to criticism. Sometimes our response will be positive and will make us want to try harder and learn more, other times criticism can leave us feeling like giving up. This is true for children and so it becomes even more important that early years educators consider how they can impact positively on young children's beliefs about themselves as learners. Often criticism is given in order to motivate a child to 'do better next time'. However it often has the opposite effect. It quells any desire to try something new. McLean (2003) suggests that information from three sources helps us to build up our personal theories about ourselves

1. Comparison with others.

2. Feedback from significant others.

3. Interactions within their own particular contexts.

Young children often view practitioners as all-knowing, and so their words are very important to them. Rather than filtering out the 'good bits' from the 'bad bits' they remember what has been said. If they hear 'I like your junk model' they may also hear 'I like you'. If they hear 'I don't like your junk model' they may also hear 'I don't like you'. These words then shape and influence the 'narrative' we have in our heads. This 'narrative' is then believed to be a stable trait, in other words, 'I can't change'. While much of this happens on an unconscious level, it is still hugely important as our words can have long-lasting effects. Work done by Heyman (1991) suggests that children who are criticized not only make general global statements about their negative traits, but also make universal decisions about the goodness of others – 'I am bad and always will be, they are good and always will be'. If we want to motivate our children to do better, then we have to think carefully about the words we use to achieve this.

## Summary

Some key points and suggestions have been made in this chapter in relation to learners and learning identity.

- Children's experiences contribute to their view of themselves as a learner.
- We need to think about how we react to children who are gifted and talented.
- Our identity depends on such things as circumstances, perception, peer reaction and confidence.
- Our beliefs about ourselves as learners will help us to better understand our approaches to and interactions with children.
- Dispositions and feelings are important in developing a learner identity.

**To think about**

- How do I deal with difference?

- How can I help to minimize the issues for gifted and talented young children and their parents?

- What do I think of my own learner identity?

- How can I help to build a positive learner identity in the children I work with?

- What words do I use when trying to motivate young children?

# How staff can support gifted young learners

Some key points about how our beliefs and theories influence how we cater for young gifted and talented learners are made in this chapter.

> - **All our actions are based on theories and beliefs.**
> - **Our beliefs and theories will influence the way we plan for learning.**
> - **We need to gather a range of evidence from a variety of sources and, based on that evidence, plan learning experiences that offer challenge and opportunity.**

## What we believe matters

All our actions are based on theories and beliefs of some kind. We may not be conscious of what these are but all that we do or say reflect in some way what we believe. Our belief about intelligence and ability can manifest itself in several ways. While we cannot avoid basing our actions in our beliefs and theories, we can examine what these beliefs and theories are, and in light of that perhaps we might even find ourselves challenging or changing our beliefs!

Consider the following conversations. What do they tell you about practitioners' beliefs and theories about gifted and talented children?

 **Case studies**

**Conversation 1**

> *Researcher:* Have you ever worked with young gifted and talented children?
>
> *Staff:* Mmmmm … I can think of one child who was good at mathematics … but I haven't worked with any recently … and certainly not in this nursery.

*(Continued)*

*(Continued)*

This conversation highlights two issues:

1. The staff member seems to associate being gifted and talented with an ability in mathematics, thus suggesting they perhaps have a narrow view as to what constitutes 'gifted and talented'.

2. The staff member suggests that the physical location, that is, post or zip code of the nursery will impact on the likelihood of finding gifted and talented children within the group.

What difference does this make to practice?

If we believe that being gifted and talented is limited to traditional notions of ability (that is, mathematics and language), then if we do provide challenging tasks they are likely to be in the traditional areas of mathematics and language. We will also fail to see, acknowledge and develop other abilities that lie beyond this narrow view.

If we believe that gifted and talented young people are only found in certain types of catchment areas then we may not look for them in our setting if our setting, for example, is in an area of deprivation, has a high number of children from an ethnic minority group, has children for whom English is an additional language or has children who have a disability. We may offer low-challenging tasks to children as we do not believe that they are capable of achieving much more.

### Conversation 2

*Parent:* I'm not sure if you want this kind of information but I just thought the nursery might like to know that she knows all her colours and can count to 100.

*Staff:* Well we have lots of children who can do things like that.

*Parent:* She's started reading too. She can read simple words. We think she's quite clever.

*Staff:* All parents think their children are clever.

This conversation highlights four issues:

1. The hesitancy on the part of the parent to divulge information suggests they may not want to be classed as a 'pushy parent' and may even be embarrassed to admit that they think their child is clever.

2. The staff reaction to being told the child knows their colours and can count to 100 suggests that there is nothing unusual in a child being able to do these kinds of things.

3. The additional information supplied by the parent might be the parent trying to suggest that their child is engaging with activities beyond what might be expected for their age.

4. The staff reaction to the parent's perception of their child's ability might suggest that they believe the parent to be holding too high an opinion of their child and what they can do.

*(Continued)*

Staff need to be constantly thinking about next steps in learning for children in their care. However, staff who 'expect' children to achieve certain activities may not always be thinking about this. When a child is doing well with the existing activities, staff can sometimes see no need to plan for additional challenge for particular individuals.

Working with parents is crucial but can be notoriously difficult! Staff who are unwilling to accept the parents' assessment of their child may go out of their way to catch children out in order to prove the parent wrong. Staff may also create a climate where parents are hesitant and unsure about raising issues regarding their child in case they are not believed, thus the setting misses out on vital information for planning. Parents bring a wealth of information that can be used to enhance the learning opportunity. While settings are right not to put young children under pressure by setting unrealistic goals, they need to strike a balance so they are collating relevant information that supports them as they plan for meaningful learning experiences.

### Conversation 3

> *Adult 1:* Look at that, he builds a beautiful model then spoils it by tipping all the blocks out of the box onto the floor.
>
> *Adult 2:* Well what do you expect, he's Jack's brother. You know what that family have been like all along.
>
> *Adult 1:* Yes, I should feel sorry for him really. He's never going to amount to much with a background like that and coming from that gene pool.

This conversation highlights three issues:

1. Being neat and tidy and following nursery rules appears to be more important than engaging with the task.

2. A comparison between siblings is made and a conclusion unfairly arrived at.

3. Children's futures can be predicted by genetic heritage.

Young children spend much of their time trying to work out what makes them 'good' and what makes them 'bad'. At the same time, staff may be, subconsciously, looking for children who comply with nursery rules. If staff associate neatness and the obeying of rules with ability, then they will seek out and highlight those young children who are conforming to this belief. They might fail to see the good work and learning achieved by someone who does not follow the rules.

If staff believe a child cannot 'get any better' due to their family and social background, they will do little to challenge any abilities a child may demonstrate. Judgements are made based on previous experiences of working with the family. All family members are presumed to be the same. Staff may have had low expectations for this child even before they arrived in the setting if they believe that background is a predictor of ability. Instead of looking at how they can support a learner, they stand by and watch things become a self-fulfilling prophecy. This emphasizes to staff how good they are at predicting the future of young people. In fact, perhaps quite a different outcome could be achieved if appropriate support were offered to children.

All these real-life conversations highlight for us beliefs and theories about intelligence and ability.

- If we believe that high ability is all down to genetics, then we will only look for it in certain children and possibly in certain socio-economic areas.

- If we believe high ability is demonstrated through competence in mathematics and language, then we will only recognize those children who are 'good at reading and counting'.

- If we believe that all children are gifted and talented and as such need the same curriculum opportunities, then we will not offer more challenging experiences to those who need it.

- If we believe parents are pushy, then we may ignore vital information that will help us to plan appropriate learning experiences.

As we interact with the children in our care, these beliefs and theories will ultimately impact on learner identity. Staff will decide who is gifted and talented and who is not, and will then plan learning experiences accordingly.

The following case studies offer an opportunity to consider this in greater detail.

 Case studies

Consider the following questions for each of the case studies provided. There are no right or wrong answers to these scenarios. You will find some suggestions at the end of each case study.

1.  What view of academic ability do the educators hold?

2.  How does their view influence their expectations of the children?

3.  How does their view influence their planning of activities for the children?

**Early years setting**

The early years setting is within an area of considerable social and economic deprivation. Some staff have worked in the setting for a lengthy period of time. Indeed, they have worked with many of the parents whose children now attend the setting. Staff refer to the children as 'no hopers', saying that they will amount to very little coming from this area, just like their parents before them. When planning learning activities, the staff members see it as their duty to ensure that the children engage in activities that will keep them occupied for as long as possible, after all, a child with nothing to do will cause trouble. Thus activities concentrate on offering children low-level challenge so they can succeed.

The underlying belief here is that intelligence and intelligent behaviours are solely dependant on biological and genetic factors. This view of intelligence often coexists with the belief that gifted and talented children do not normally come from socially and economically deprived backgrounds. Success in the setting will be influenced by these set features. Effort and learning experiences will not be part of the equation. While genetics, biology and areas of social and economical deprivation impact on learners and learning, they do not have the last word. These beliefs in turn impact on staff expectations for the children. In the setting in this case study, children are not expected to be successful learners. They will be expected to achieve an acceptable level of basic education but at the end of the day they are going to turn out like their parents. Where such a view is held, staff will not have high expectations for children and in turn, children will not have high expectations, goals or aspirations for their future. If staff believe genetics have predestined some children to 'fail' and if they believe that children are not capable of achieving much due to genetic composition, then the activities on offer will be of low-level challenge. If we see all children as 'equal', staff may shift the focus from learning to behaviour. Creating challenging learning experiences should contribute to a purposeful ethos within the setting. Where this is established, behaviour ceases to be the focus with learning taking centre stage.

**Danger:** A child in this setting who is gifted and talented may be overlooked as no one is expecting to find them there!

### Roaa, age 4 and a half

Staff within the setting hold regular meetings to discuss individual children's progress. One member of staff regularly flags up Roaa who although quiet, has shown particular ability in the design process. It has been suggested that as Roaa has particularly good spatial awareness, can see things in both two dimensions and three dimensions and can read maps, particular activities should be designed for her to encourage this ability. The majority of the staff think that only children who have been tested and who display advanced abilities in mathematics and language should be offered tailored educational experiences. Roaa, they believe, needs to become more interested in literacy and numeracy activities. After all, this will provide her with a good grounding for formal schooling.

Some staff within the setting believe that academic ability can be measured. This measuring will usually be done through norm-referenced tests or through specific tests designed by the setting. In addition, mathematics and language are the focus of such tests as it is in these areas that a gifted and talented child will shine. However, one staff member has a broader view of intelligence and as such seeks to offer challenging learning opportunities in a variety of curricular areas. These beliefs about ability go on to influence staff expectations. For some staff, success is dependent on the 'basics' being in place and abilities outside the area of mathematics and language do not have to be challenged. For the other staff members, a more holistic, all-round approach is adopted, leading to a possible rise in expectations for all. These differing expectation levels influence what happens in the setting. Some children have to prove they are competent at something staff value before they receive challenge and even then, due to the hierarchical view of curricular areas, that challenge will only be offered within mathematics and language. Abilities that occur in other areas remain unrecognized and therefore unchallenged. For the staff member who holds a wider view of ability, offering challenging learning experiences becomes difficult as colleagues share such differing views.

*(Continued)*

*(Continued)*

**Danger:** Children's abilities will go unnoticed and unchallenged as there is a narrow view of what constitutes ability.

### Lauri, age 3

Shortly after arriving in the setting, Lauri has demonstrated particular ability in mathematics, being able to add, multiply, subtract and divide. An individual programme of work has been put in place for Lauri and she spends much of her time working on this or the computer. Staff are keen to ensure that the mathematical ability is developed to its full potential as the majority of parents are 'professionals' and expect this kind of programme.

This case study challenges a number of commonly held assumptions about ability. As in the case with Roaa, there is an underlying belief that you can in some way accurately measure ability. The fact that staff are keen for her to reach her full potential suggests this. There are perhaps some difficulties with the notion of 'full potential' – how do you know when someone has reached it? What happens when you reach it? Potential suggests that there is no end, so to suggest you can reach full potential seems to inhibit learning rather than encourage it. In addition, the evidence presented certainly seems to suggest Lauri has learned some computational processes however, this is one aspect of mathematics and quite a limiting and narrow view of mathematics.

Where these beliefs are in place, we can again see that success in this setting is dependent on the 'basics' being in place. Staff also seem to assume that her computational ability means she will be capable of following a narrow programme of work. The planning of activities for Lauri are led by the parents' perceived expectations, with little consideration given to developing wider aspects of mathematics. Individual or computer-led activities are offered with little opportunity for interaction with others and no provision is made to challenge the child's holistic profile alongside her ability in computation.

**Danger:** The development of the child's mathematical ability is not rounded due to the concentration on computation.

### The early years setting

Staff work on the basis that all children are gifted and talented and as such they provide a wide and varied programme of activities and visits. All children participate and observations are made and recorded. Regular feedback is given to carers and full notes are passed on to the next educational establishment.

In this setting, staff hold a very wide and all-encompassing view of ability. Ability is not confined to the traditional notion of academic ability. There are some strengths to this approach; however, the staff's collective expectations may be high or low. Observations may be general and, as such, miss vital information about children and their learning. When this happens no provision will be made to challenge a child's particular abilities as they may have been missed. All children are given the same opportunities, but when this is accompanied by general observations it may lead to little individualization of the curriculum.

**Danger:** While there is much to be said for a wide view of ability and a wide range of activities being on offer, treating all children in the same way may lead to those with particular abilities being overlooked.

## A different view of ability

We have seen how beliefs and theories can impact on learner identity in a negative way. Let us consider how beliefs and theories can positively impact on learner identity.

Consider the following conversations. What do they tell you about people's beliefs and theories about ability and children?

 **Case studies**

**Conversation 1**

> *Researcher:*  Have you ever worked with young gifted and talented children?
>
> *Staff:*    Mmmmm … yes. I've come across some children who can do amazing things for their age. Even children from pretty awful area status can constantly surprise you.

This conversation highlights two issues:

1.  The staff member is acknowledging that ability might not be dependent on or related to age.

2.  The staff member suggests that the physical location, that is, post or zip code of the nursery, has nothing to with whether or not you will find gifted and talented young learners.

Moving away from the traditional idea that ability is linked to age will help us to look for latent abilities rather than a perceived norm. If we believe that gifted and talented young people are found anywhere, then we will be looking for them regardless of our geographical location. We may offer challenging tasks to all children as we believe this will offer children an opportunity to demonstrate what they can do. Observation becomes crucial, as we need to be looking for the abilities children demonstrate through the opportunities so we can then challenge these existing abilities.

**Conversation 2**

> *Parent:*  I'm not sure if you want this kind of information but I just thought the nursery might like to know that she knows all her colours and can count to 100.
>
> *Staff:*  That's really useful to know.
>
> *Parent:*  She's started reading too. She can read simple words. We think she's quite clever.
>
> *Staff:*  It is great she's showing an interest in print. We'll bear this in mind as we plan activities.

This conversation highlights four issues:

1.  The hesitancy on the part of the parent to divulge information suggests they may not want to be classed as a 'pushy parent'.

*(Continued)*

*(Continued)*

2.  The staff reaction to the first piece of information reassures the parent that this is useful information for the setting know.

3.  The additional information supplied by the parent might be the parent trying to suggest that their child is engaging with activities beyond what might be expected for their age.

4.  While not agreeing that the child is 'clever', the staff member has acknowledged that an interest in print is important and they will use this information when planning for learning opportunities.

Gathering information about children from a range of sources, including home, allows staff to plan meaningful learning experiences for children. Parents and carers see children in a range of situations and they can help staff to gain a broader sense of what the whole child is like. Key to this is building up positive relationships with parents. This is vital if home and the setting are to work together and we are to move away from parents being concerned about sharing information about learning and particular abilities. Where staff are thinking about next steps and additional challenge for particular individuals based on what the child can already do, they will be keen to collaborate with parents.

**Conversation 3**

*Adult 1:*  Look at that, he's built a beautiful model and then tipped all the blocks out of the box onto the floor. It is not quite what we wanted him to do but I wonder why he did that?

*Adult 2:*  His brother would never have spent time building a model like that.

*Adult 1:*  It is interesting to see how different they are although they are from the same family.

This conversation highlights three issues:

1.  Staff need to look beyond actions to understand why children do certain things.

2.  A comparison between siblings is made but not necessarily in a judgemental way where one sibling is considered 'better' than the other.

3.  Staff acknowledge that being from the same family does not mean everyone will behave in the same way.

While staff are keen to understand the unexpected action of tipping out the blocks the focus is on why this happened rather than on the fact it would have been better not to have happened. Staff acknowledge the hard work and effort that have gone in to the building of the model in spite of the tipping out of the blocks, learning is still the main focus, not behaviour. Although staff have knowledge of the family, they do not use the information to pre-judge the child and more importantly do not compare the child to their brother.

All these scenarios highlight for us beliefs and theories about intelligence and ability.

-  If we believe high ability is not all down to genetics, we will look for the possibility of it being present in a number of children.

- If we believe high ability is not restricted to post or zip codes, we will be looking for children in all walks of life.

- If we believe high ability requires effort, then we will acknowledge when children expend energy and effort in tasks.

- If we believe high ability is more than being good at mathematics and language, we will look beyond the traditional curricular areas for evidence of it.

As early years educators interact with the children in their care, these beliefs and theories will ultimately impact on learner identity. Practitioners will gather a range of evidence from a variety of sources and, based on that evidence, they will plan learning experiences that offer challenge and opportunity.

The following case studies offer an opportunity to consider this in greater detail.

 ## Case studies

Consider the following questions for each of the case studies provided. There are no right or wrong answers to these scenarios. You will find some suggestions at the end of each case study.

1.  What view of academic ability do the educators hold?
2.  How does their view influence their expectations of the children?
3.  How does their view influence their planning of activities for the children?

### The early years setting

The early years setting is within an area of considerable social and economic deprivation. Some staff have worked in the setting for a lengthy period of time. Indeed, they have worked with many of the parents whose children now attend the setting. Staff work hard to ensure that all children in their care are offered a range of experiences across the curriculum, thus laying the foundation for successful learning. They are also ready to spend time with children who have not had, for example, rich language experiences prior to coming to the setting. They are keen to work from 'where the child is at'.

Within this setting it is acknowledged that all children deserve the opportunity to engage in and with challenging learning experiences. Staff accept that different children require different support depending on previous experiences. Crucially, they recognize that children have to be seen as individuals. Staff in this setting will expect children to engage with learning. Having engaged children in learning, they are expected to continue learning and to develop their abilities. Where this view of learning is in place, children are seen as individuals and the starting point for planning is finding out what that individual can already do. This results in a range of cross-curricular opportunities that will be offered to all.

**Opportunity:** Providing a rich learning environment and offering support for children will allow for abilities to emerge.

*(Continued)*

*(Continued)*

### Roaa, age 4 and a half

Staff within the setting hold regular meetings to discuss individual children's progress. One member of staff regularly flags up Roaa who, although quiet, has shown particular ability in the design process. It has been suggested that as she has particularly good spatial awareness, can see things in both two dimensions and three dimensions and can read maps, particular activities should be designed for her to encourage this ability. At first staff were unsure how to structure such activities. Two members of staff offer to research this and report back to the group, having sourced information on the Internet and through books. They have also enlisted the help of a parent who works in the creative design industries.

Staff in this setting hold a broad view of intelligence and are willing to recognize abilities beyond mathematics and language, thus the creative aspect is not ignored. Having recognized an ability in a child, staff realize that the child is capable of more than they are already displaying; thus expectations are raised. Planning learning experiences for this child becomes a collective responsibility and talking together will allow information to be drawn together from a variety of sources. It is acknowledged that some kind of differentation of curriculum may be necessary to challenge this child. Althought staff are not sure how to plan next steps for learning, information is sought from books, the Internet and from people with knowledge of the area under consideration. In this setting, the teacher is viewed as a co-learner. Working as a team to plan learning for one individual will create better learning opportunities for all.

**Opportunity:** Abilities beyond the traditional view are acknowledged and team working ensures abilities will be challenged.

### Lauri, age 3

Shortly after arriving in the setting Lauri has demonstrated particular ability in mathematics, being able to add, multiply, subtract and divide. An individual programme of work has been put in place for her and she spends much of her time working on this or the computer. Staff are keen to ensure that the mathematical ability is developed as the majority of parents are 'professionals' and expect this kind of programme. However, they also want to make sure all children experience a wide range of activities and that all aspects of mathematics are woven into curricular areas.

While mathematical activity is focusing on computation, there is recognition that children require a range of mathematical experiences in the setting. Staff are keen to ensure the child is challenged at a level appropriate to the child's abilities and expectations are influenced by the expectations of parents. Thus, individual programmes of work that take account of computational abilities are implemented. However, opportunities to integrate mathematics into other curricular areas are sought and planned for. This goes some way to ensure that mathematics is considered in its widest sense.

**Opportunity:** Cross-curricular opportunities offer meaningful, real-life experiences for all children and take mathematics beyond the 'more difficult sums' approach.

### The early years setting

Staff in the setting work on the basis that all children are gifted and talented and, as such, they provide a wide and varied programme of activities and visits for the children. All children participate and observations are made and recorded. Staff expect all children to do the best they can. Regular feedback is given to carers and full notes are passed on to the next educational establishment.

Staff seem to hold a very wide and all-encompassing view of ability. This results in ability not being confined to the traditional notion of academic ability where emphasis is placed on mathematics and language. There are collective expectations with staff expecting the best from all. All children are given the same opportunities, which is valuable as abilities may develop. Careful observation has an important part to play here, as has communication between the setting and home. The passing on of information offers opportunity for progression in learning but is dependent on the receiving establishment understanding the wide view of ability that has been adopted.

**Opportunity:** Having challenging material for all may mean gifted and talented learners will engage rather than switch off. It will also allow for emerging abilities to develop and be challenged.

In the early years high ability, and children's beliefs about high ability, will be evolving. We can impact on these negatively and positively, and much will depend on what we believe about high ability. We may find we have to rethink long-held positions on high ability if we want to challenge and nurture the young children in our care.

 Summary

Some key points and suggestions have been made in this chapter in relation to beliefs and theories.

- We are all influenced by our beliefs and theories about learning and intelligence.
- Our beliefs will impact on how we work with children.
- We need to be aware of what we believe and perhaps be willing to change our beliefs if necessary.

 To think about

- What do I believe about intelligence?
- How my beliefs about intelligence impact on my practice?
- Do I need to rethink what I believe about intelligence?

# 3

# Learner stories

Some key points about the personal stories of gifted and talented learners are made in this chapter.

> - **There are several myths about gifted and talented children that need to be challenged.**
> - **We need to look at the evidence to destroy the myths.**
> - **There are a number of narratives or stories to be found in every early years setting.**
> - **Children will behave and act according to 'their story'.**
> - **Some narratives will clash and some will dovetail.**
> - **We need to have shared narratives and understandings so we can support gifted and talented young children.**

There are a number of myths around about gifted and talented children. Let us consider what some of these myths might be.

Gifted and talented children:

- are 'loners' and have trouble fitting into their peer group

- are gifted and talented in all areas

- are immature

- are always easy to work with

- can be identified through intelligence tests and academic achievement

- are self-motivated

- are well behaved

- are not good at sports

- are always recognizable in the early years

- do not need help; they will do very well on their own

- always exhibit immature social behaviour

- are all high achievers

- know where they are heading

- do not have problems; they will handle them on their own.

While *some* gifted and talented children may display *some* of these characteristics, they are by no means common to all. If we buy into any of these myths they will influence the way we work with the children in our care. These views can then become the dominant narrative or story about gifted and talented children in our settings.

Let us consider the first myth that gifted and talented youngsters are 'loners' and often have trouble 'fitting in' to their peer groups. Chronologically, they are the same age as their peers but they may not be the same age intellectually. When this mismatch happens children can feel isolated, lonely and, occasionally, find themselves rejected by the group. Contrary to popular belief, I would suggest these children are not immature but are, in fact, very mature. However, let us see how a belief in this myth might influence what we think about a child and how we react to a child. Consider the following case study.

 **Case study**

The sign at the sand says 'No more than five children at the sand tray'. Five children, including a gifted child, are happily playing in the sand when child number six arrives.

The gifted child tells child number six they cannot play in the sand. Child number six ignores this advice and continues playing. The gifted child becomes agitated and says loudly, 'You can't play here, look, it says no more than five and you make six'. This too is ignored by child number six.

The gifted child becomes upset and points to the notice saying, 'But you can't play here just now, you have to go away'. Child number six becomes fed up with this and lashes out at the gifted child. The gifted child in turn lashes out at child number six who lets out a yell and begins to cry.

What do you think happened next?

**What happened next**

The early years practitioners hear the commotion and turn around in time to see the gifted child lashing out with his fists. They intervene, removing the gifted child and telling him if he cannot play nicely at the sand, then he is not playing at all and really they expected better behaviour than this from him. The practitioners then discuss how immature this boy is and how he is unable to mix and play with his peers.

Up until the point where he lashed out, the gifted child was in fact behaving quite maturely. He had read the sign, counted the number of children at the sand tray, remembering to include himself and was obeying the setting rules. He was helpfully telling his peer that he was not obeying the setting rules. However, this is misinterpreted by staff who only observe the end of the incident and staff conclude the gifted child is immature, unable to form friendships or connect with others and cannot work cooperatively. From this one incident he could receive three labels:

1. gifted – he could read the sign.

2. fair/just – he was following the rules.

3. badly behaved/violent – he hit another child.

Each label would have a totally different outcome for the child, resulting in totally different baggage which will follow him around. While in some ways the conclusion reached is an understandable one based on what they saw, as practitioners we need to look beyond the immediate situation and consider alternatives.

Now consider this case study.

 ## Case study

The same gifted child meets with pupils from the associated primary school. Together they work in the nursery garden. The pupils have brought different types of soil for the children to work with and they look up reference books and the World Wide Web prior to planting the seeds. The gifted child works cooperatively with the older children to record information, use this information to decide which seeds they will plant in which soil and where they will plant the seeds for maximum growth. He works with his age peers as they plant and water the seeds, with each child taking on a role and working as part of a team to finish the task.

Here we see our gifted child working with a group of older children as well as his peers. When he is actively engaged in appropriately challenging tasks and is working alongside intellectual peers, he displays a number of skills that would refute the earlier claims that he is immature and cannot make friendships with others. It is also interesting to note that when gifted children have the opportunity to work with like-minded peers they will often become more confident in engaging with their age peers. As practitioners we should now have a very different view of this child.

> ## Points to remember
>
> - Gifted and talented children are unlikely to be immature. They may simply require like-minded individuals to work with.
>
> - We should always consider what may be behind a particular behaviour; it may not always be as simple as we first think.
>
> - Working with intellectual peers can help a gifted child to work more comfortably with, and have more understanding of, their age peers.

## Perception is a wonderful thing

A psychologist called Jerome Bruner (1996) considered the importance of the idea of narrative or story. Narrative helps us to understand ourselves and the world in which we find ourselves. Narratives can be traced back over the centuries – Romans told of their gods, Christ used parables, and Australian Aboriginals told of their Dreaming. These narratives were powerful instruments and could engender compassion, change lives and incite action. Today, stories continue to be important, especially in the areas of interpersonal relationships, personal and social advancement, and learning. Some suggest they are as important as the food we eat because we just cannot imagine life without stories. Each culture or community will have a range of stories that help us to understand ourselves better through listening to the stories of others.

In an early years setting we are familiar with the importance of storytelling. Storytime is often the highlight of a child's day. A child can lose themselves in a story – think of the fairytale 'Jack and the Beanstalk' – they really are Jack, they really have climbed the beanstalk, they really are fighting the giant.

The children you work with may have a whole narrative or story built around them. Indeed they may have built a narrative around themselves, for example, 'I am not clever, but I am popular. I can make people laugh …' They can come with 'baggage' and/or a 'reputation'. As educators, we get caught up in a particular story or narrative about the child and as a result of this we spend little time exploring other aspects of the child and their life – alternative narratives. We buy into the story and sometimes we add to it. I visited a nursery once and was met by a 3-year-old boy. The following conversation ensued:

> *Child:*  Hello, what's your name? I'm the bad boy.
>
> *M:*    My name's Margaret, do you have another name?

At this point the child skipped off and spent the rest of the morning showing me just how bad he could be and therefore why he had received this name. In other words, if our understanding of ourself is wrapped up in a particular story then we have to prove how we fit the story. This is true for some gifted and talented children. They have to:

- show us how smart they are

- get everything right all the time

- be finished first or,

- be the best.

Narratives or stories affect us as adults too. We all have personal narratives about ourselves. Let us think about this in relation to our ability to cater for gifted and talented learners in our care. Your narrative may be influenced by:

- your ability to devise and develop appropriate tasks

- previous experiences of devising tasks

- how you will be perceived by colleagues/parents

- your confidence (or lack of it)

- your success

- how good you are at risk-taking.

Running parallel to your personal narrative is a dominant narrative. This is shaped by the official expectation of the event. This will have been determined by your line manager, the education authority (EA) and legislation. Where these three narratives dovetail, then there are likely to be few problems. But when the narratives are at odds, then difficulties can arise. If you are worried and concerned about your ability to cater for gifted and talented children, and yet you know that parents, staff in the school and the EA expect you to be doing this effectively, it will impact on how you approach your work.

Alongside our personal narrative, the child's narrative and the dominant narrative, we have the parents' narrative. They too will have a story. They may be concerned and worried about their child. They may believe the setting sees them as 'pushy parents'. They may be really struggling to know how to deal with this young child who already knows as much as they do about chemistry. Parents will come to a meeting with staff with certain feelings and expectations as a result of these stories, and this will result in them behaving in a certain way. Consider this true experience told to me by a parent:

> The setting is really hung up on getting him to sit still and form his letters correctly and go through the whole phonics programme. They can't get him to sit still for 5 minutes of phonics but I have seen him not move a muscle listening to a 45-minute lecture on the nature of light and its relevance to the space–time continuum.

We essentially have a series of narratives and stories that come together in our settings. Some of them will clash with each other and some will dovetail together. In an early years setting the educators' response to the narratives and stories that people have is crucial in ensuring a positive outcome for all concerned. As

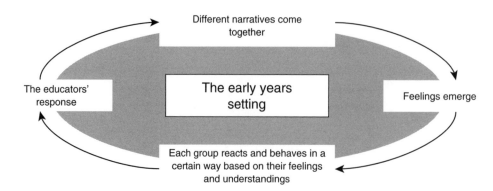

**Figure 3.1**   The early years setting

educators, we need to be aware of the cycle that exists (see Figure 3.1) and, where tensions arise, we need to look for ways to break them.

When the educator responds in a way that helps all the stories to emerge, then the experience will be better for everyone.

We can see that understanding narratives or stories about ourselves, the children, parents, colleagues and the work setting will help us to better understand the situation we find ourselves in. Once we understand where the clashes are (see Figure 3.2), we can go about finding ways of reducing those (Figure 3.3).

With all children, there is potential for conflicting narratives and understanding. Table 3.1 helps us to see what some of these might be in relation to a child who is gifted and talented. We will look at a situation from three perspectives:

1. The child.

2. The parent.

3. The early years educator.

We will also consider how this links to what we know about gifted and talented children. While it is dangerous to generalize, there are common themes which occur in the literature and when speaking to children and parents.

Looking at Table 3.1, we can see how different stories about the same situation occur. We work with a large number of children and therefore some of the situations that cause difficulties in the setting cause no such problems outside the nursery, when the child may be with an adult in a one-to-one situation. We therefore have to be open to looking at circumstances from different viewpoints. Seeing things differently will help us to think differently about things. Sharing our understandings will also help parents, as well as ourselves, to see the child from a different perspective. If we have a greater understanding of what life can be like for gifted and talented children, we can begin to appreciate why children, and adults for that matter, do or say certain things in certain situations. Let us consider how we can support the child.

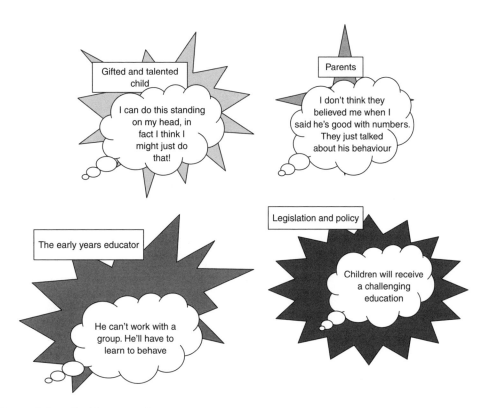

**Figure 3.2**     Clashing narratives

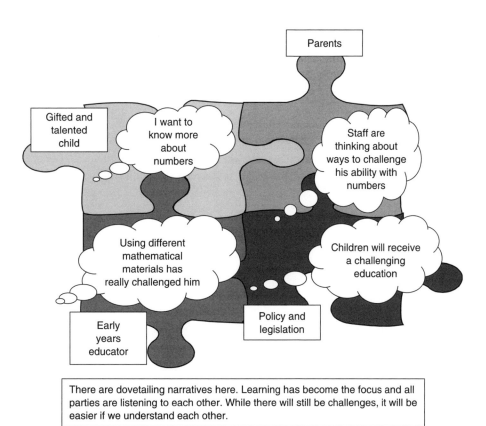

**Figure 3.3**     Dovetail narratives

**Table 3.1   Situation chart**

| | The situation | The child | The parent | The early years educator | How this links to being gifted and talented |
|---|---|---|---|---|---|
| 1 | Doesn't like working in groups. Prefers to play independently | No one here understands what I'm saying. They can be so slow to work things out I just have to do it for them | She only plays with her cousins. They're older than her but they get on really well | This child is not good at turn-taking. She always bosses the other children around and tells them what to do. She needs to learn to work as part of a group | Gifted and talented children can find it hard to relate to their age peers and need an intellectual peer. Their peers don't think at the same level or quickly enough for them |
| 2 | Always asking questions. Wants to know details | There's just never enough information about things. I always have to ask for more. Sometimes things are made to sound easy when they're not, they're complicated | He never stops. He finds it hard to go to sleep because his mind is so active | He is always asking questions. It can become quite annoying when you're working with others. Sometimes I can't answer them | A high level of curiosity is often present. Children want to gain in-depth knowledge and are genuinely interested in how things work and why. They can often have trouble switching off |
| 3 | Wicked sense of humour evident | No one laughs at my jokes. I don't think they get them | She has an adult sense of humour. She can have us all in stitches | She can be quite funny but sometimes it's bordering on being cheeky. She doesn't know how to relate to adults | Again the child can be operating at a different level from their peers and will often make connections and see things from an adult perspective. They can prefer adult company |
| 4 | Becomes upset when listening to certain music or discussing certain topics | I can really feel the pain animals and people feel. It makes me very sad | He is a very sensitive child. He gets upset quite easily | He bursts into tears easily. He can be quite immature | Some children can have a heightened sense of justice and injustice and can care very deeply about social issues. They have strong feelings and emotions |
| 5 | Lashes out at peers. Never really engages with activities. Is only interested in dinosaurs and numbers | I hate it when I have to play with others. We play silly counting games. I know all that stuff. I get fed up with the others | I'm concerned about her behaviour. She's becoming more withdrawn at home and doesn't want to look at books or play games anymore | She will have to learn to work alongside others and do all the activities on offer | When a child is not challenged appropriately they can become bored and frustrated. This will often manifest itself in inappropriate behaviour |

## Does not like working in groups; prefers to play independently

We can begin by asking an adult to play in parallel with the gifted child, with the expectation that the child will eventually converse with the adult to give the play some direction. The adult should accept the invitation to play cooperatively, following the child's lead. This offers the adult an opportunity to use more sophisticated vocabulary, ask more complex questions and engage in more complex dialogue. The practitioner may also introduce the child to a wider range of resources and materials to support their interest. When the relationship (this may take a period of time to develop) is established, the practitioner can then introduce a carefully chosen peer to interact with the gifted and talented child. The peer might be one who is interested in the same topics, has complementary skills or who has good social skills.

## Always asking questions; wants to know details

A child who constantly asks questions can become quite draining on the practitioner. In addition, it can begin to affect confidence if a gifted and talented child is constantly asking questions to which you do not have answers. The practitioner can help children to frame questions by asking the child to think of their three best questions. The child can ask these questions at the end of the session. At the beginning of the following session, the adult and the child can together source answers to the questions posed. This approach encourages the child to think about asking quality questions. If the wrong questions are posed, then the answers will not satisfy the child's demand for knowledge. It also forces the child to prioritize their thoughts so that they ask the most pressing questions first. By asking the child to pose the questions and leaving some time prior to answering them, both the child and the adult can investigate possible answers. Research skills are being developed; one person is not seen as the keeper of knowledge. Richer discussion is more likely to occur if both the child and the adult have approached the questions as co-investigators. The process of arriving at an answer is as beneficial as the answer itself. Learning how to source information to solve puzzles, questions and problems is a valuable skill for all young learners to acquire.

## Wicked sense of humour evident

We will all be able to think of jokes that make us laugh and others that do not. There is not a universal blueprint for sense of humour. Humour can be culturally based. Humour can also be sophisticated. It is perhaps this sophisticated humour that the gifted and talented child can tap into. Being able to 'read between the lines', to understand nuance or a play on words will all help the gifted and talented child to appreciate and engage in humour that their peers will not have begun to understand. If the practitioner has formed a relationship with the child and knows the child well, then they will be able to discern between 'cheek' and the child's natural sense of humour.

## Becomes upset when listening to certain music or discussing certain topics

Gifted and talented children can often empathize deeply with others. It is being able to make an emotional attachment to people, situations and feelings that means children can have a heightened reaction to emotional moments. It is well documented that music can stimulate a range of emotions in individuals. Thus it can trigger a reaction such as tears or anger, and cause them to become unsettled. When this happens the adult has to support the child by offering opportunities to vent these feelings. This might be through discussion, painting or composing their own music as a response.

## Lashes out at peers; never really engages with activities; is only interested in dinosaurs and numbers

Gifted and talented children often become bored with regular, repetitive activities. While other children require over-learning and repetition of skills, gifted and talented children do not. Although not always the cause, gifted and talented children may lash out as a result of being bored in these situations that are not challenging enough to hold their attention and cultivate their thinking and learning. They may become frustrated by their peers because they have surpassed that stage of learning. It is essential that practitioners find out what children can already do. If a child has an understanding and interest well in advance of others, then tasks and learning outcomes need to be relevant and personalized.

To fully understand children in our care, we have to gather information from a range of sources. This will help us to see a situation from other standpoints. These should inform our understanding and challenge our preconceived ideas. Ultimately it should help to support children in our settings.

## Where do we go from here?

In the first three chapters we have looked at:

1. Our own learner identity.

2. Our beliefs about gifted and talented children.

3. The importance of shared narratives or stories.

Before we plan any activity we need to have developed our thinking in each of these areas. This will leave us in a better position to consider how we go on to provide challenging activities for gifted and talented young children.

The next chapter looks at activities that will allow us to develop and nurture each child's learning identity.

Summary

Some key points and suggestions have been made in this chapter in relation to narratives and stories.

- We need to be aware of our own narratives and stories in relation to gifted and talented children.

- We need to recognize and appreciate the personal and dominant narratives of children, parents, colleagues and legislation.

- We need to seek to minimize the clashing of narratives.

 To think about

- Have I bought into some of the myths about gifted and talented young children?

- Do I look for the underlying meaning of some behaviours?

- How often do I explore the narratives that surround situations, people and children?

# 4

# Creating challenge for gifted young learners

Some key points about how we can create challenging activities for young gifted and talented learners are made in this chapter.

- **Activities work best when they relate to children's interests and take account of what children already know and can do.**
- **Challenge needs to be built in at the planning stage.**
- **A story can be a good starting point for developing activities.**
- **Cross-curricular topics offer good opportunities.**
- **It is important to find out what children know before you start a topic.**
- **Displaying children's work offers good learning opportunities and values the contribution each child makes.**

Creating challenging activities is easy to say but can be hard to do. What exactly does 'challenge' mean? Will a 'challenging activity' for one child be a 'challenging activity' for another?

The word 'challenge' has many meanings. The original meaning comes from the old French, *chalenge*, meaning accusation, claim or dispute, and from Latin, *calumnia*, meaning trickery. Since the 1980s, the term 'challenged' has been used in connection with appearance and physical characteristics, such as vertically challenged. A person can challenge someone to a round of golf. They can call something into question and challenge someone's beliefs. In an educational context, the word is usually used when referring to a task that will stimulate by presenting the child with difficulties which they have to overcome.

How, then, can we build in challenge to our curriculum? Valsa Koshy (2002) worked with teachers and considered what it meant to offer challenge. They came up with three factors that would ensure challenge in the curriculum. She suggests it is useful to remember to include activities which:

1. Relate to children's own interests. These are likely to increase their motivation and encourage them to make their best efforts.
2. Offer a meaningful context for the work.
3. Are placed just above the child's capability to tackle the task and fulfil the requirements. While a task which makes cognitive demands at an unrealistically high level may lead children to give up easily, tasks which require little effort will often be seen as pointless, and lead to boredom and frustration.

(Koshy, 2002: 37)

The flexibility and responsive nature of the early years environment seems an ideal place to allow us to meet the needs of gifted and talented children and, indeed, all children.

---

! **Points to remember**

When creating an environment to challenge and stimulate, remember to:

- create a space that invites enquiry by having a wide range of materials available

- plan time for free choice areas of study

- change the atmosphere in the setting through, for example, music

---

Gifted and talented children will have an array of interests. Some children are gifted and talented across a number of areas of the curriculum and others are gifted and talented in particular areas. If we plan cross-curricular activities we can go some way to ensure we 'catch' the interest of as many children as possible. We can offer children opportunities to develop existing skills and abilities as well as offering opportunities to discover new skills, abilities and interests.

Think about the broad areas of learning you develop. Look at *some* of the characteristics that *some* gifted and talented children display, in Table 4.1. Can you think of children who display some or all of these characteristics?

**Table 4.1   Characteristics**

| Characteristic |
| --- |
| High intellectual curiosity |
| Learns quickly in one or more subject areas |
| Constantly asks questions |
| Vivid imagination |
| A non-conformist |
| Displays great empathy/sensitivity |
| Keen sense of justice |
| Excellent verbal ability |
| 'Adult' sense of humour |
| Highly creative |
| Has high ability but lacks motivation |
| Divergent and/or lateral thinker |
| Tends to be a perfectionist |
| Rapid learner |
| Perseveres at a task that interests them |
| Can concentrate for lengths of time on something they are interested in |

While there may be other factors that influence how a child interacts with learning, if you have a child who displays some or all of these characteristics then it might be indicative of a child who requires challenge.

 **Cross reference**

Page 40 has a photocopiable sheet you can record your observations on. These can be used to help you gather evidence and plan activities.

**Child's name** _____

**Key worker** _____

**Date** _____

| Characteristic | Evidence |
| --- | --- |
| High intellectual curiosity | |
| Learns quickly in one or more subject areas | |
| Constantly asks questions | |
| Vivid imagination | |
| A non-conformist | |
| Displays great empathy/sensitivity | |
| Keen sense of justice | |
| Excellent verbal ability | |
| 'Adult' sense of humour | |
| Highly creative | |
| Has high ability but lacks motivation | |
| Divergent and/or lateral thinker | |
| Tends to be a perfectionist | |
| Rapid learner | |
| Perseveres at a task that interests them | |
| Can concentrate for lengths of time on something they are interested in | |

## Linking learning across the curriculum

Our starting point can be used as a springboard into a range of curricular areas and can offer us an opportunity to observe the wide variety of abilities they may present.

I use stories as starting points for activities which will challenge children across the curriculum. The activities suggested here are inspired by a story called *How to Catch a Star* by Oliver Jeffers (2004) and published by HarperCollins. However you could relate the activities to almost any other book about stars.

Before you begin, here are some practical ideas for storytelling:

- Read the story several times before you read it to the children.

- Practise using different accents and registers for different characters, but use these sparingly throughout the story for maximum effect.

- Practise intonation, speed and volume.

- Be ready to respond to the 'audience's' reactions.

- Plan where you will stop and ask questions or ask the children to predict what happens next.

- Make sure the children are sitting comfortably; big cushions are ideal.

- Ensure children can see the pictures as you read.

- Make eye contact with the children as you read.

- Encourage the children to interact with you and the story.

- Enjoy performing the story and then your audience will enjoy listening!

 Storytelling activity: stars

- Gather the children round for storytime. Make sure the children are comfortable and can see the book. Introduce the book. Discuss the name of the author, illustrator and title.

- Read the book to the children. Involve the children in the story. Can they predict what will happen next? Do they understand any unusual words? Make sure that you help the children to 'read' the pictures. This will help the children to create a narrative from the clues the pictures provide.

- When reading the book, make sure you offer time for the children to make connections between the book and real life.

- Highlight for children the conventions of storytelling, such as beginnings, endings and problems in the plot.

- Where children can read the text, let them join in with the telling of the story.

While practitioners can frame questions about the story, the story itself may leave the children asking a range of questions. Taking the lead from the children is more likely to result in the children being motivated to investigate and extend the ideas.

**Table 4.2   Focus area for language/communication**

| Communication, language and literacy | Knowledge and understanding of the world | Emotional, personal and social development |
| --- | --- | --- |
| Recognize the link between the written and the spoken word | Begin to understand the idea of time | Natural curiosity |
| Understand the language and layout of books | Natural curiosity | Sense of wonder |
| Use language for a variety of purposes | Sense of wonder | Concentrate for lengthening periods when involved in appropriate tasks |
| Listen to a good story | Ask questions | Respond positively to a range of new cultural and linguistic experiences |
| Ask questions and listen to responses | | Develop sensitivity to the needs of others |
| Express opinions | | Make and express choices, plans and decisions |
| Identify and explain events illustrated in pictures | | |

### Extending the topic beyond the story

Taking your lead from the children, build on their knowledge and interest. A number of possible routes into exploring, for example, scientific concepts, may emerge from stories about stars.

Practitioners I worked with identified possible areas and topics for development around the central theme of stars, including:

- colour
- weight
- texture
- shape
- sequence
- weather

- the night sky, for example, shooting star
- stars
- transport
- space and planets
- shadows
- reflections

- shiny and dull
- night and day
- illustrator's use of colour
- problem-solving

- water
- sound
- measure distance
- time

Cross-curricular opportunities abound here. Learning cannot be seen in discrete subject areas. Helping children to make connections between subject areas through a central theme, such as stars, is vital if children are to make connections between learning experiences.

Many children, including gifted and talented children, are interested in stars and space, and are fascinated by the sky. Using a story as a starting point, the practitioner can offer young children the opportunity to investigate astronomy, something that becomes a lifelong passion and interest for many.

## Displaying children's work

Finding out what children already know about a topic before we start will go some way to ensure that we do not offer repetitive information and activities that reinforce what children already know rather than taking forward their learning. Displaying this information at the start of a topic will allow children the opportunity to think about what else they would like to know. It also allows staff to see what direction future learning and planning will take.

As practitioners we need to think how displaying work helps us to:

- enhance and develop the children's learning

- celebrate children's different abilities

- encourage further thinking

- create a context that motivates children to want to know more.

We need to think carefully about why we want to display children's work. While it shows visitors and parents what the children have been doing in the setting, there are other sound educational reasons for displaying children's work. It can be difficult if your setting does not have a permanent meeting place. In this case, you have to be a little more imaginative as to how you display work. You could use movable features such as free-standing boards, airing racks, strong storage boxes or boxes on wheels. Even when it is challenging, it is important to display children's work.

Displaying children's work helps the child to:

- feel part of the community that makes up the early years setting

- think more deeply about the topic covered

- feel their work is valued

- make connections between the different concepts being discussed

- interact with the learning opportunities.

If the work has been done in the outside area or if a model has been made, photographs can be taken and displayed or made into a CD-ROM.

 **Cross reference**

The photocopiable chart on page 45 allows you to record what the children already know about:

- stars

- the sun

- space

- planets.

## Ideas for how to display children's work

1. Create a wall space where all work will be presented. Ideally this should be at child height so children can display and see their work. This bank of information will act as a record of the work covered and will also allow practitioners to see the development of the children's ideas and understanding. It can be used as a reference point and children can refer to the wall for information. It is continuous and ongoing.

2. Tables or strong boxes should be arranged at differing heights. These can be covered with fabric and used to display three-dimensional work.

3. The children should come up with a name for the wall/floor space but it could be called:

   (a) All about stars

   (b) Sparkling star stuff

   (c) Stars, solar systems and constellations

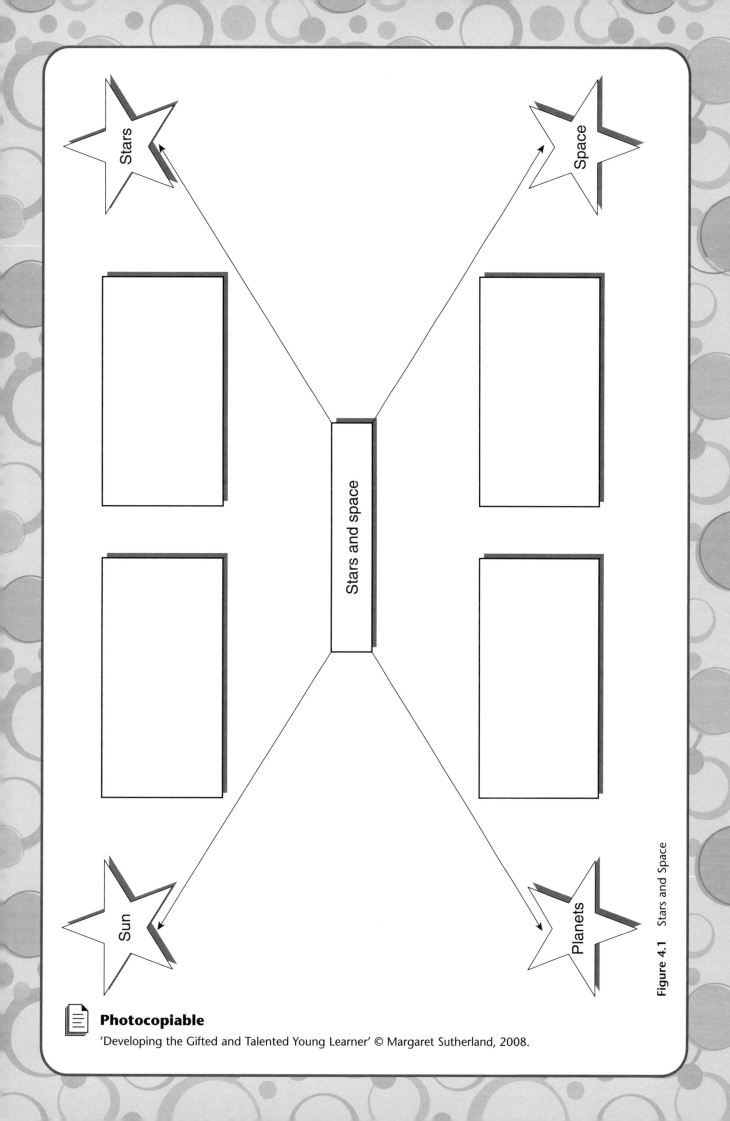

Stars

Space

Sun

Planets

Stars and space

**Figure 4.1** Stars and Space

4. Show the children pictures of stars. These can be collected over a period of time from magazines, books, the Internet, and so on. Pictures can also be downloaded and put together into a montage on a CD. This can be shown accompanied by background music such as *The Planet Suite* by Holst. Viewing this in a room that is slightly darkened will add to the atmosphere. Children can be asked to bring pictures of stars from home.

5. Establish what the children already know about stars. Record this information on the wall. Information might include:

    (a) They are seen at night.

    (b) They sparkle.

    (c) They look as though they have pointy edges.

    (d) They are made of gases.

    (e) They are far away.

    (f) You look at them through telescopes.

6. This kind of information can be recorded pictorially or on a CD as well as in written word format so that the children can refer to it as the work continues. Pictures and/or words could be stuck onto star shapes before mounting them on the wall. To create a space feel to the work, background colours for the display should are likely to be black or dark blue, and fabric used should reflect the space theme – it could be dark, shiny with moons, stars and planets on it. Children should suggest which colours and fabrics can be used for backing displays.

7. Fiction and non-fiction books should be available for children to browse.

8. Fact cards can also be made. Each card contains a fact about space, the sun, stars, and so on. The fact can be written or pictorial. They could be written in the form of a question with the answer under a flap. This allows the children to speculate as to what the answer might be. These can be added to as the topic develops.

Materials you will need to gather as you plan and develop your topic might include:

- Black or dark coloured backing paper for the wall. Milskin is ideal for this.

- Different kinds of shiny/sparkly materials, for example, paper, material, glitter, off cuts, sequins.

- Left- and right-handed scissors.

- Pictures of stars and space to be used as stimulus for ideas and discussion.

- Labels.

- Tables of differing heights or strong boxes of differing sizes.

- Fabric.

- Fiction and non-fiction books of varying levels of difficulty.

Now you know what the children already know about stars you can start to plan activities that will take forward their learning and understanding. This new knowledge will be added to the display as the topic develops.

## Summary

Some key points and suggestions have been made in this chapter in relation to developing activities for gifted and talented young learners.

- We need to think about challenge from the planning stage.

- We need to find out what children already know about the topic.

- We need to display children's work in a way that develops their learning and values their knowledge.

## To think about

- Do I plan across curricular areas to engage and challenge children?

- Do we have stories that can offer a good basis for cross-curricular work in the setting?

- When I display children's work, does it add to the learning experience?

## Further reading

Factsheets about stars, the sun and space exploration and a glossary of space terminology are included in the Appendix. They are to be used as guide or a starting point for the practitioner.

Jeffers, O. (2004) *How To Catch A Star.* London: HarperCollins.

# 5

# Activities for gifted and talented young learners

Some key activities for young gifted and talented learners are offered in this chapter.

- **Early years education seeks to offer a broad learning experience for all.**
- **The early years educator's role in the learning experience is crucial.**
- **Learners need to be involved in their learning.**
- **Gifted and talented children need to use their energy and enthusiasm to explore and experiment.**

## General guidelines for early years settings

We should be aiming to create an enriching learning environment for all. When we look at national documentation across the four nations that make up the UK, we discover that they are all concerned with the same things. They do not always use the same terminology, but ultimately they all seek to develop:

- emotional, personal and social development

- communication, language and literature

- knowledge and understanding of the world around us

- expressive, aesthetic and creative development

- physical and movement development

- mathematics, problem-solving, numeracy and reasoning.

These broad areas of learning give us a good framework as we seek to design and develop challenging activities for children.

A key issue acknowledged nationally by each of the four nations is the role the early years educator plays in developing learning, but perhaps the most difficult things for us as educators is to know when to intervene and when to stand back. Many of the studies about early years learning (for example, Pascal et al., 1996; Siraj-Blatchford and Sylva, 2002) discuss this very issue. It is hard because our own involvement with the activity has to be considered alongside the involvement of the child. Nevertheless, despite this difficulty, actively involving young children in their learning is an important strategy in the early years setting. So how do we ensure an appropriate balance between child led activities and adult led activities?

In the early years children are constantly trying to make sense of their world. Bruner (1996) suggests that to do this they will be connecting what they know already with the new ideas and knowledge they meet. If we use this as a starting point then the adult has to:

1. Ensure they are providing a wide range of resources across the curriculum for indoor and outdoor play.

2. Ensure they organize resources in such a way that they are attractive, easily accessible and flexible.

3. Involve the children in the organization of materials, for example, deciding where areas should be set up and naming the areas.

4. Ensure children can move resources around independently.

5. Plan experiences that stimulate interest.

6. Build in the opportunity for children to revisit and re-examine work, thus leading to deeper understanding and confidence-building.

7. Watch and evaluate how the children interact with the resources. This is crucial if further planning of opportunities is to be meaningful and to meet children's needs.

8. Interact with the children thus modelling situations; however, the adult then has to allow the children to explore further independently (Sutherland, 2006: 13).

We also have to think about all this in relation to a child who is gifted and talented. While what we do might be the same for every other child, we need to be aware that a gifted and talented child's starting point is different. We also need to be aware that gifted and talented children often love to investigate for themselves. We must avoid 'shoe-horning' children into particular activities where, despite the appearance of choice, it is in fact severely restricted. Remember also that a gifted and talented child can sometimes focus on a single task for lengthy periods of time. They often return to the same activity/equipment time and time again. This in-depth play is important to their development.

The mother of a gifted and talented child said: 'He loved to use the toys for his own imaginative play when the staff only wanted him to use them for the purpose it said on the box. I don't know if they felt he wasn't learning if he didn't use them for the proper purpose.' Creativity is often a hallmark of someone who is gifted and talented. It is much more likely to be evident through the process of an activity. A child who is gifted and talented can often see endless possibilities, outcomes and alternative solutions to activities. We need to observe children in more depth in order to gain a real understanding of their learning. As practitioners we have to be ready to allow gifted and talented children to use their energy and enthusiasm to explore and experiment.

Points to remember

To sum up, early years staff need to:

- become a partner in the learning process
- be flexible in the outcomes and routes taken to those outcomes
- be ready to allow the child freedom to experiment and choose activities
- engage in open-ended questioning
- give formative feedback
- channel the child's energy and enthusiasm into exploration and experimentation.

Let us look at some ideas that we can develop and adapt to suit our settings. Remember I have used a story about stars as a starting point, and so I have picked up on the theme stars and space. The above guidance, however, can be used to plan any topic for study and you can use different topics as starting points for development.

*Note:* The following activities can be used with all children in the setting. However, they offer opportunities for gifted and talented young children to explore in greater depth some of the concepts from a story.

 Star activities

1. Children can be introduced to the common constellations to be found in the hemispheres. They will only see the stars above the hemisphere in which they live. Using a globe, locate the country they live in and establish which hemisphere it is in.

2. Children who live in built-up areas should discuss light pollution and how this affects our ability to see stars. Children can look for constellations at night. The children can record their findings on the photocopiable sheet on page 54. Many different constellations fill the night sky. Your location and the season will affect which ones you can see.

3. Children may also enjoy looking for other patterns, real or imagined, that they can see in the night sky. They can record these. This work can be added to the space wall.

4. Many of the names of the constellations relate to Greek mythology. Retell the stories. The children can dramatize these, create collages, make puppets and re-enact them.

5.  Have the children make up their own names and stories for the constellations.

6.  Some children will know about meteors and may even be concerned about a large one landing on them. Care should be taken when talking with children about meteors, and their concerns should be taken seriously. Gifted and talented children are often very worried about the world and can often feel helpless to change things. Couple this with a scientific understanding of meteors and this could leave a young gifted and talented learner feeling very insecure. The children could investigate where meteors have landed. They could investigate impact by dropping, from varying heights, spherical and other objects which could represent meteors into damp sand or water.

7.  People have been studying the stars for thousands of years. The children can find out about ancient civilizations and their studies of the stars. These civilizations include:

    (a)  the Babylonians

    (b)  the Egyptians

    (c)  the people of Stonehenge, UK

    (d)  Chinese astronomers

    (e)  Mayan astronomers.

8.  Although we can see a lot of stars with the naked eye, we really need equipment to help us see details. Children should be given the opportunity to look through binoculars and hand-held telescopes. Children should also be given the opportunity to experiment with different lenses, introducing the idea of concave and convex lenses. While it is unlikely to be dark when the children are in their setting, they can practice with equipment

    **Warning!** It is dangerous to look at the Sun with the naked eye. Children should be told about this.

9.  The children can be introduced to the Italian, Galileo, who was the first astronomer to use a telescope to look at the stars, and to the Dutchman, Hans Lippershey, who built the first telescope in 1608.

10. The Hubble space telescope orbits the Earth, taking photographs of the universe. The following Internet link allows the children to see pictures taken from the Hubble space telescope: www.hubblesite.org.gallery.

11. The children can build their own telescopes and binoculars from junk materials. Having gathered information from books, the Internet and magazines about telescopes, their models should be as accurate as possible. Make sure a range of materials is available for the children. You could include:

    (a)  cardboard tubes

    (b)  plastic tubes

    (c)  sticky tape

    (d)  wires

    (e)  cellophane – different colours

    (f)  glue sticks

(g)  string

(h)  ruler

(i)  set square

(j)  protractor.

Advice on buying astronomy equipment is available at: www.seasky.org/astronomy/astronomy_ equipment.html.

12.  The children can bake star-shaped biscuits. This offers an opportunity for discussing the real shape of stars. When we see stars in the sky, they are small and seem to twinkle, hence the famous children's song 'Twinkle, Twinkle Little Star'. Of course they do not really twinkle and they are not really small. Air currents in the Earth's atmosphere makes the starlight bend. Some of the light reaches our eyes, some is bent away from our eyes. This makes them appear to twinkle. The recipe on page 55 can be printed out on cards and laminated so the children can follow it.

**Draw the constellation you can see**

**Use your imagination. Can you see any other creatures or shapes in the sky? Draw them here**

## Star biscuit recipe

### You will need

Mixing bowls

Measuring spoons

Start-shaped biscuit or cookie cutter

Whisk or mixer

Rolling pin

Baking sheets

Self-sealing plastic bags

### Ingredients

8oz or 227g butter

1 cup icing sugar/powdered sugar/confectioners sugar

1 cup cornflour/cornstarch

2 cups plain flour/all purpose flour

Put on oven at gas mark 4/350 °F/180 °C

### Method

1. Cream butter and icing sugar in bowl.

2. Add sifted cornflour and plain flour and mix well.

3. Roll out mixture on a surface until ¼ inch/0.6cm thick.

4. Cut into star shapes using a star-shaped biscuit/cookie cutter (or you can make your own template out of paper).

5. Place biscuits onto a baking tray.

6. Bake in the oven for 15–20 minutes until golden brown.

7. Allow to cool.

8. Decorate with coloured icing sugar, vermicelli, etc. (optional).

9. Store in self-sealing plastic bags … or eat and enjoy!

**Photocopiable**

'Developing the Gifted and Talented Young Learner' © Margaret Sutherland, 2008.

## Sun activities

1.  Using models or even fruit to represent the Sun and the Earth, explain how the Earth moving around the Sun means that at times part of the Earth is in darkness and so we can see the stars in our galaxy, at other times the brightest star is closer to us and so it outshines the other stars. Moons travelling around planets can also be added.

2.  The Sun's energy comes from the core. Children can explore how the energy travels outwards from the centre. Dropping a stone into a bucket of water and watching the ripples will allow children to visualize the process. Some children will be ready to use the correct terminology for the process (see the factsheet in the Appendix for details).

3.  Blow up a large balloon. Cover it in papier mâché. Make the surface jagged and rough. Paint the surface with yellow, red and orange paint. Remember to include darker patches for sunspots. Experiment with different medium so that the surface looks 'alive'. For example, mix a little Polyfilla into the paint and this will allow the children to form peaks on the surface. Add pipe-cleaners to the surface to represent explosions on the Sun's surface. Use tissue paper, coloured shiny paper, and polythene to represent plasma loops. The children can suggest materials that can be used.

    **WARNING**: Do not put the paint and Polyfilla down the sink or drains as it will harden and block them.

4.  The children can make a number of papier mâché 'suns' which can be fitted inside one another to make a cross-section of the Sun, showing how the energy escapes.

5.  Gather information about how to stay safe in the Sun. Talk about protecting our eyes by never looking directly at the Sun and always wearing sun cream when we are outside in the sun. Children could bring in sun glasses and sun cream.

6.  The Sun provides energy for the Earth. Many people have thought of the Sun as a god. The children can find out about, for example, the Mayan people in South America.

7.  The children can explore what happens to the Earth when the Sun shines and there is little rain. The impact of this on food production, availability of water and so on can be discussed. Newspaper and magazine articles about drought can be brought into the setting and discussed. It should be noted that 'too much sun' does not just happen in 'hot' continents such as Africa. Southern England had a shortage of water in 2006.

8.  A globe and lights can be used to explain the Earth rotating.

 ## Space exploration activity

1.  Man has landed space robots on Mars, Venus, the Moon and the asteroid, Eros. Some space robots move about to find out more, others stay still. The children could discuss what kind of information they would want to find out from the space robots. They could build space robots from junk material or from construction materials that would help them to gather this information, for example take pictures. They could make models using simple technology so they actually move.

2.    Children can re-create the surface of a planet from papier mâché and tactile materials. They can place their space robots on the surface. The planet surface could be a re-creation of an actual planet visited by a space robot or they could invent a planet. Roamer can be programmed to move across the surface of the planet.

3.    The children can explore what conditions have to be present on a planet to sustain life as we know it, for example, liquid water, energy such as the Sun, nitrogen and carbon. This will help them to better understand our own planet, Earth, as well as discover which planets might have the right conditions to sustain life forms.

4.    Landing on a planet can be a dangerous time for space robots. The children can experiment with landings by attaching parachutes to their space robots and dropping them from various heights. Discussions about gravity will also follow from this. You can find out more about a failed landing by looking for information on the landing of the Genesis capsule in 2004 in the desert in Utah.

5.    The children can turn the home corner into the inside of the International Space Station (ISS). The children should investigate what will be required to live in space, for example, special food, clothes, and so an. They should think about how they will communicate with Earth while they are there. They should plan out the ISS and set it up. While you will not be able to re-create the effects of zero gravity, discussion can take place as to what this would be like. See the list of useful websites at the end of this book which help children to understand what living in space is like.

6.    Experiments can be carried out in your ISS. For example, you could grow seeds under different conditions – no light, no water, light but no water, water but no light, and so an.

7.    Particular skills are required of astronauts, for example, quick reaction times, hand–eye coordination, good memory. Games can be played outside and indoors that help to develop these skills. Children can devise games and create an astronaut school which will train astronauts before they go to the ISS. See also the website list at the end of this book which helps children to develop skills.

8.    The first rockets were not powerful enough to reach space. The children can experiment making rockets. They need to consider the shape of their rocket – this will introduce them to the idea of aerodynamics. Trajectory can also be explored. These kinds of experiments will require adult supervision.

9.    Nowadays, trips into space take place on the space shuttle. The children can compare traditional rockets with the shuttle. Questions they might explore could include:

(a)    Why does the space shuttle have wings? Experiments can be carried out as to how wing span affects flight.

(b)    Why does the space shuttle look more like an aeroplane than a rocket?

(c)    Do the astronauts on the space shuttle do the same things as the first astronauts in space?

10.    For children who are particularly interested in numbers, they can explore the idea of light years. The nearest star is over 4 light years away. The centre of

our galaxy, the Milky Way, is 30,000 light years away. The nearest Galaxy is 2 million light years away. Children can explore the idea of looking back in time – since objects are so far away, looking at distant objects means you are actually looking back in time!

11.    Gravity is a force that pulls things together. Children can experiment with different sizes of objects and gravity, thus exploring the concept of mass.

## Summary

Some key points and suggestions have been made in this chapter in relation to activities for gifted and talented young learners.

- We need to think about challenge from the planning stage.

- The practitioner is a learner in the process too.

- Children have to be involved in their own learning.

- Children need to explore and experiment.

## To think about

- How often do I involve children in their own learning?

- When do I allow children to explore and experiment?

- Does the layout of the room/building put constraints on what we can do?

## Further reading

Dowswell, P. (2005) *The Usborne Little Encyclopedia of Space*. London: Usborne.

Kerrod, R. (2000) *Questions and Answers: Stars and Planets*. London: Kingfisher.

Stott, C. (2005) *Stars and Planets*. London: Kingfisher.

# Inclusive provision for gifted young learners

Some key points about how we can offer challenging activities to young gifted and talented learners in an inclusive setting are made in this chapter.

> - **Provision needs to be considered before identification takes place.**
> - **Learning and learning potential should be the focus during identification.**
> - **Our beliefs about learning and ability will influence how we interpret information.**
> - **Incidental, specific and collective observations will allow us to plan for challenge.**

## Approaches to identification

Identifying gifted and talented children can be problematic. The traditional approach to identification means that we identify a group of children using particular criteria. Often these criteria are based on a limited view of what ability means and unsupported evidence and impression. We then label the children, in this case with the label gifted and talented, and then we provide appropriate activities for them. There are some difficulties with this as we will see.

## Traditional approach

Identification ⟶ Provision ⟶ Support ⟶ Challenge

When we identify using this approach, we are looking for what children can already do and often this is skills based. Once we see them demonstrating these skills we provide practice/resources which may not always be the most appropriate next step for learning. We will then work alongside this identified group, offering support and challenge when we feel it is appropriate.

## An example of planning for gifted and talented children using the traditional approach

Identification   *I am looking for children who:*

- grip their pencil well

- know their sounds and can read simple words

- know their numbers to 20.

Provision   *I will make available:*

- opportunities to begin writing letters, for example, their name

- simple addition sums

- activities for blending sounds together.

Support   *I will:*

- help them to form letters correctly

- read books with/to them

- talk to them about environmental print.

Challenge   *The children will:*

- be offered lots of opportunities to develop writing skills

- be offered opportunities to practice number concepts

- practice rhyming words

- have access to simple books in the library.

## Difficulties associated with this approach

- Identifying the child often relies on the educators' understanding of ability/gifted and talented.

- We only offer opportunities to those already demonstrating ability/gifts and talents.

- We may only identify in a narrow/traditional range of subjects/abilities such as mathematics and language.

- Having identified the narrow area, we continue to give practice in it.

- Abilities and skills demonstrated in, and valued by, the early years setting become the focus of identification.

Wherever we are working, we are likely to be working within some kind of framework that sets out what children will achieve before they move on to the next stage of their learning. Often these frameworks are concerned with school learning goals. These goals would include:

- Colouring in within the lines (that is, 'neatly').

- Using scissors (without looking as though they might stab themselves or someone else).

- Writing their name independently (for example, on their artwork).

- Recognizing numbers (for example, from environmental print).

- Reciting the numbers 1–20 and beyond.

- Knowing some letter and sound names (for example, 'what sound does your name begin with?').

- Knowing which way to hold a book (when in the library corner).

- Knowing how to turn over the pages of a book.

- Knowing that print reads from left to right (Sutherland, 2005: 20).

While these skills are important and should be developed, success in these are not necessarily an indicator of a child who is going to 'do well' at school nor of a gifted and talented child. However, we often gather this kind of information about a child and, on the basis of this and our beliefs about intelligences (discussed in Chapter 2), make assumptions about a child's readiness to learn. Consequently, we tailor learning opportunities accordingly.

If we accept that the search for ability in the early years is, by its very nature, a search for emerging abilities, then we have to adopt a different approach from the traditional model we have just discussed. Identification through provision would seem to offer a more holistic and inclusive approach.

## A holistic and inclusive approach

Provision   ⟶   Identification   ⟶   Challenge   ⟶   Support

While we are using the same words as the traditional model, we have changed the order in which we use them. Starting with provision means all children can be offered the opportunity to demonstrate what they can do. It also means that we are able to begin to identify a range of abilities that children might display and adjust provision accordingly. While a child might well demonstrate the skills used for identification in the traditional approach, the holistic and inclusive approach broadens these concepts and contexts to enable deeper levels of thinking to be demonstrated. Perhaps most importantly, it allows for the identification of children beyond the traditional areas of mathematics and language.

Provision    *All children will be offered the opportunity to:*

- investigate solid shapes

- explore uses for Lego

- experiment with mark-making equipment

- read a variety of fiction and non-fiction books.

Identification    *I will be looking for children who:*

- manipulate ideas

- make connections between subject areas

- think logically

- can communicate their ideas

- recognize patterns

- attempt to link sounds and/or read

- concentrate for long periods of time.

Challenge    *The children will:*

- investigate the relationship between solid shapes made of glass or clear material and light

- build intricate three-dimensional designs using Lego

- write stories using words and pictures

- read for meaning – this could be linked to a specific task.

Support    *I will*

- ask open-ended questions

- look for multi-level outcomes

- offer information when it is required

- encourage children to reflect on their work.

This approach offers opportunities to:

- observe all the children in a range of contexts

- cast the net wide in terms of identification

- look for children who approach activities in creative and unexpected ways

- discover children who deliberately add challenge to tasks to make them more interesting

- scaffold the children's learning who are not yet ready to complete the tasks independently.

Learning and the potential for learning become the focus. Learning dispositions or learning habits become important. The holistic and inclusive model is about identifying in order to challenge learning at a specific time, and not about assigning a particular label to a child.

## Gathering information

Much of the evidence we can use to identify gifted and talented children in an holistic and inclusive way can be found in our setting. We just need to know what to look for and how to interpret it. Think about the space and star activities discussed in Chapters 4 and 5.

### Possible things to look for

- Can read the book.

- Has an in-depth scientific knowledge about stars and space.

- Can use reason and logic when suggesting answers.

- Is empathetic to other children's knowledge, suggestions and ideas.

- Can articulate ideas succinctly.

- Uses complex words and sentences.

- Uses facial expression and body language to communicate ideas.

- Asks questions.

- Dissatisfaction with simplified explanations and insufficient detail.

- Can be very focused.

- Enjoys researching and applying scientific theories, ideas and models.

- Analyses data or observations and spots patterns easily.

- Sees the big picture.

- Misses out steps when working out the answers to problems.

- Can predict.

- Enjoys talking to the practitioner about new concepts or ideas.

- Presents original, sometimes off-the-wall, ideas.

- Has joined scientific clubs or hobbies outside of the setting.

- Is inquisitive about how things work and why things happen.

This is not an exhaustive list and as you observe the children you may become aware of other things they are doing that suggest there is some deep learning taking place.

## The role of observation

In the early years setting, there will be various ways you already observe children's progress. These could include:

- tracking individual children

- observation of individual children for a specific purpose

- recording individual children's learning in a specific area

- incidental observation.

Your setting is likely to be divided into activity areas, for example, malleable, painting, role play, jigsaw, sand/water, outdoor. These areas offer ideal opportunities for staff to observe children participating in a range of activities. These observations can then be collated in order to inform planning, support and challenge for specific children.

 Cross reference

The photocopiable sheet on page 66 will support staff as they make their observations. There is a sample in Figure 6.1.

Staff will have observed children at different times of the day in different contexts. We now need to gather the information from observations and use it to inform future planning for individual children.

**Figure 6.1**   Science/space corner

**Area: science/space corner**

**Week beginning: 15 October**

**Key Worker: Pia Kopwe**

| Date | Child | Significant observation |
|---|---|---|
| 29.10.07 | Fraser D | Spent 20mins experimenting with concave/convex lenses |
| 29.10.07 | Euan S | Asked why lenses are different shapes |
| 30.10.07 | Karen C | Visited science area for first time – mention to mum |
| 30.10.07 | Fraser D | Experimented again today with both types of lens. Looked at the effect on objects |
| 31.10.07 | Fraser D | Spent almost 25 minutes in area. Drew what the pen and teddy looked like through both lenses. Wrote teddy and pen below pictures |
| 31.10.07 | Euan S | Looked through lenses at objects FD was interested in |
| 1.11.07 | Niamh P | NP said teddy looked fat through one of the lenses (convex) |
| 1.11.07 | Fraser D | Explained what was happening to NP. Used correct terminology regarding lenses and light. Also described the teddy as 'distorted vision' |

**Area:**

**Week beginning:**

**Key worker:**

| Date | Child | Significant observation |
|------|-------|-------------------------|
|      |       |                         |
|      |       |                         |
|      |       |                         |
|      |       |                         |
|      |       |                         |

 **Photocopiable**

'Developing the Gifted and Talented Young Learner' © Margaret Sutherland, 2008.

We now have information about children in a range of contexts. We need to use the evidence we have to identify children who are ready for the next steps in our holistic and inclusive model: challenge and support.

>  **Cross reference**
>
> By pulling together our observations, we can build up a picture of a child's learning and from this plan next steps. An example has been completed in Figure 6.2. The photocopiable sheet on page 68 will allow you to plan for individuals.

Remember, much of this information is already in the setting. It may be a case of simply changing what you look for and then using this to plan for challenge and support.

**Figure 6.2**   Planning for individuals

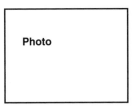

| Name:  Fraser Don |
| --- |
| Age: 3½ |
| Key worker: Ross Hunter |

| What we ... | Notes |
| --- | --- |
| observed | • Experimenting with concave/convex lenses<br>• Noticed effect of different lenses on objects<br>• Recorded his observations pictorially and in words<br>• Correct use of technical language |
| decided to do | • Add binoculars and a telescope to the science/space corner to see if Fraser would develop his understanding of lenses and the effect of differing lenses<br>• Help him to record his observations in a systematic way |
| then observed | • Fraser worked out convex lenses held near an object made it look bigger because the lens bends the light rays inward<br>• Fraser completed the charts for his observations. He was keen to add information regarding distance of objects<br>• Fraser brought a magnifying glass from home and added this to the artefacts in the science/space corner<br>• Fraser started to ask questions about contact lenses |
| decided to do next | • Introduce Fraser to the images from the Hubble telescope<br>• Encourage Fraser to design his own charts for recording purposes<br>• Add non-fiction books about the eye and how it works to the library<br>• Introduce the idea of light years to capitalize on Fraser's interest in distance |

| Photo | Planning for individuals |
|---|---|

| Name | |
|---|---|
| Age | |
| Key worker | |

| What we ... | Notes |
|---|---|
| observed | |
| decided to do | |
| then observed | |
| decided to do next | |

## Photocopiable

'Developing the Gifted and Talented Young Learner' © Margaret Sutherland, 2008.

## Gifted and talented children with multiple exceptionality

While we can plan, provide, observe and identify, there is still the possibility that we will overlook some children. These children can escape our attention for a variety of reasons. One such reason is that the child may in fact have what is referred to as 'multiple exceptionality'. This refers to the fact that a child may have another label that is masking their gifts and talents. Educational settings tend, understandably, to focus on the label requiring some kind of intervention often neglecting to notice that the child is also gifted and talented and this too requires intervention. In many ways we need to be like a detective. We need to gather clues and then consider what they mean for next steps in learning. The following case studies will help you to reflect on the learning needs of individuals.

 Case studies

### Georgina

Georgina's family have caused the setting concern for some time. There are social issues which means that mum/dad are not always focused on the needs of their children. Georgina often arrives late and misses the morning routine and instructions. Staff have spoken with the parents about this but so far there is no evidence of things improving. Georgina is unkempt in appearance. Some of the other children have accused Georgina of 'smelling' and they refuse to sit at the same table as her. Understandably this upsets Georgina who then lashes out – swearing and thumping the other children. In an effort to stop this aggression towards others Georgina spends a lot of her time alone and separated from her peers. This way not only can Georgina get on with the activity in hand but the others can peacefully engage in their learning too. However, there continues to be problems with aggression when the children are in the yard during outdoor play.

Academically Georgina is about average in mathematics and language development, and academic ability is not causing particular concern. She shows exceptional curiosity in the world around her and is always asking questions. However, staff describe Georgina as a 'ball of anger' and as such are concerned that Georgina will 'explode' at any minute. Staff are considering what behaviour strategies to put in place, for example, reward charts, time out, home/school diary recording misdemeanours, circle time.

The only time Georgina seems focused and relaxed is during investigative and problem-solving activities. During these times the aggression seems to disappear and she becomes fully engaged in the activity. Staff are unsure whether Georgina could work as part of a group during these times. Staff find Georgina's continual asking of questions draining and often they are unsure how to answer the questions. It is possible that this constant questioning would put off other children in the group were they to be working in a group situation, and so Georgina remains working on her own.

**Table 6.1**   Case study 1

|  | **Georgina** |
| --- | --- |
| Causes for concern | 1. Late arrival in setting<br>2. Personal hygiene<br>3. Verbally and physically aggressive<br>4. Finding appropriate behaviour strategies |
| Positive learning attributes | 1. Performing as expected for her age<br>2. Exceptional curiosity in the world around her<br>3. Can focus when problem-solving or engaging in investigative tasks<br>4. Asking questions |

 Case study 1

It is possible that a two-pronged approach is required here:

1. Continuing work with the family, perhaps involving social services or some kind of support services if they are not already involved.

2. Developing a learning plan that takes account of and starts from Georgina's abilities.

Practitioners often focus on areas other than learning. Frequently, we will have limited success in changing areas of a child's life that are outside our control, such as in the family, home or community. We can, however, ensure that children receive an appropriate learning experience in our setting. The setting should acknowledge the difficulties a child may be facing and accept that these may well affect their readiness to learn. Nevertheless, the setting should consider the learning attributes a child displays and build on these. While the learning attributes above do not necessarily mean the child is gifted and talented, there are some indicators that she requires more challenging learning experiences. For Georgina, the setting might consider the following:

1. Opportunities to explore the outdoor area with an investigation bag, for example, magnifying glass, bug catcher, small spade, plastic containers for collecting samples, microscope.

2. Provision of natural materials for experimentation and investigation, for example, bark, bricks, wood, soil, sand, grass, mud.

Initially these tasks could be carried out alone, carefully observed by a member of staff. This should allow the staff member to plan responsively following the interests of Georgina's learning. The staff member should also use careful judgement as to how and when to interact with Georgina. It may by appropriate for the adult to co-investigate. Encouraging Georgina to share her findings with other children will allow staff to locate others with similar interests. These children can then become involved in future investigations.

**Derek**

Derek has been causing staff concern for sometime now. On one level Derek is 'doing well'. He is already reading fluently, is beginning to write his own stories, will listen to story tapes with great enthusiasm and be able to discuss them at length with adults in the setting. No other child in the setting has shown such interest or ability in the written and spoken word. However, staff are extremely concerned that Derek has great difficulty in working as part of a group. Indeed, Derek will take himself to the book corner and happily read a book rather than participate in activities with others. Staff have tried to encourage Derek to work with one or two other children but this usually ends with Derek shouting at the other children and becoming frustrated when his ideas are not adopted by the rest of the group.

Staff have tried to engage in discussion about the situation with Derek but Derek is very reluctant to give eye contact or to discuss feelings. If staff continue to ask questions Derek will resort to 'hand flapping' and 'knuckle biting' leading to complete refusal to 'join in' any activities and instead will seek the safety of the book corner, often lying in a foetal position.

Discussions with Derek's parents indicate that he can have outbursts at home and, to combat this, his parents admit that they often resort to letting him have his own way.

**Table 6.2** Case study 2

|  | **Derek** |
| --- | --- |
| Causes for concern | 1. Cannot relate to his peers<br>2. Will isolate himself from others<br>3. Unwilling to discuss feelings<br>4. Does not give eye contact<br>5. Getting his own way at home |
| Positive learning attributes | 1. Can read fluently<br>2. Good fine motor skills – writing<br>3. Can write simple stories<br>4. Articulate (when he wants to be) |

 Case study 2

If we are gathering clues about the child, then this case study presents us with interesting evidence. There are clearly behaviours here that have strong links to autistic spectrum disorders – hand flapping, knuckle biting, lack of eye contact, not relating to peers and unwilling to discuss feelings. There are similar characteristics that

*(Continued)*

*(Continued)*

children with Asperger's syndrome and gifted and talented children might display. This, of course, means it is difficult to distinguish between a child with Asperger's syndrome and a child who is gifted and talented. Thus these are issues the setting would want to explore. However, there are other clues here that this child also has particular abilities. The setting needs to consider how to challenge Derek in his learning regardless of any label he may have or receive in the future. Activities could include:

1. Derek retelling a story to an adult.

2. Providing a range of books in various styles and genres. This should include poetry, non-fiction, and so on.

3. Stories that can be retold with alternative endings.

4. Using information from the text, Derek could draw a character from the text.

5. Providing a variety of mark-making tools.

6. A computer language programme where he could create stories.

While issues around socialization have to be explored, the starting point for Derek is ensuring he has access to appropriate and varied materials and learning opportunities that offer challenge and interest. Once he is engaging well with the activities on offer, other issues such as working with others, talking with others and accepting that he is part of a group can begin to be addressed.

## Summary

Some key points and suggestions have been made in this chapter in relation to holistic and inclusive provision for gifted and talented young learners.

- A common but less helpful model of identification is the traditional approach of identify, provide, challenge, support.

- An alternative is the holistic and inclusive model for identification based on provide, identify, challenge and support.

- Our beliefs and attitudes will affect how we use the information we gather.

- Existing records within the setting, for example, incidental observations/ area observation records/tracking records offer a good starting point for provision and planning.

- Consider the possibility that one label may mask a child's abilities.

- Gather clues and use the information to plan together for challenge.

To think about

- Which model of identification do I follow?

- What evidence and information is already in the setting?

- How can I pull this information together and use it to plan effectively?

- Might there be children I am missing because of my approach to identification?

- Do I actively think about children with multiple exceptionality?

## Further reading

Montgomery, D. (2003) *Gifted and Talented Children with Special Educational Needs: Double Exceptionality*. London: NACE/David Fulton.

# 7

# A framework for feedback

Some key points about the kind of feedback that supports learners and helps to create a positive learner identity are made in this chapter.

> - **Feedback is a crucial part of the learning process.**
> - **What we say impacts on the learner.**
> - **The way we say things will also impact on the learner.**
> - **Feedback needs to be specific.**
> - **Parents and staff need to work together to support young learners.**

## Feedback

Feedback is a crucial part of the learning and teaching process. It is the part that lets children know how they are doing and if they are meeting the setting's expectations and goals. The most commonly used form of feedback is oral feedback. It is instant and can send strong messages to children. Of course, through this feedback we can send negative as well as positive messages to children about their ability and therefore it is vital that we consider carefully what we say.

You may well be the key person providing this feedback. However, we should remember that the children will also have received feedback from parents, relatives and peers. It has been suggested that the kind of language experiences a child is exposed to in the home will greatly influence their beliefs about themselves as learners. By the age of 4 some children will have heard 700,000 'good things' about themselves in contrast with others who will only have heard 100,000 'good things'. This frequency impacts on the child's beliefs about themselves as a learner. Often the feedback children receive is comparative in nature. In other words, they are constantly compared to their peers, their siblings or other relatives. This can result in those who are struggling becoming more disheartened and those who are gifted and talented becoming self-satisfied. We need to consider what kind of language we will adopt in our own setting that will ensure that all children become confident learners.

We need to think about general, sometimes 'off the cuff', remarks we make to children. In particular, adults can sometimes speak to gifted and talented children in a way that suggests the child needs 'taken down a peg or two'. Much of what we say to children will be linked to what we believe about them as learners.

Let us consider what some of the negative statements we use might be.

'That's a silly idea, you know that's impossible.'

'If I had wanted it done another way, I would have asked you to do it another way.'

'What were you doing when I explained all that? Sleeping?'

'We don't have time for that right now.'

'For someone who is such a clever clogs, you can do silly things sometimes.'

'So you tried the difficult jigsaw and didn't manage it, not so clever after all then.'

'You'll do it because I said so.'

'I don't care what you think, just do it like I said.'

If we use these kinds of statements the child will feel that they are not acceptable as they are. If a child hears these sorts of comments repeated over time, it will impact on their general well-being and emotional development. We are, of course, not superhuman and we may, from time to time, become frustrated with a child or a situation. When we feel frustrated, we are less likely to take care with our choice of words. When this happens, we should be ready to apologize to the child and to explain how we are feeling and why we made the comment.

Alongside all this, we need to consider 'how' we say things to children. It has been suggested that we take in 55 per cent of our information from facial expression, 38 per cent from tone of voice and only 7 per cent from the words we say. While I am arguing here that the words we use are important, even more important are the tone of voice and posture we adopt as we say them. It is no use saying

## I'M NOT ANGRY!

if at the same time you shout it loudly through gritted teeth with your eyes narrowed, your brows furrowed and your fists clenched!

## Feedback on activities

In a busy early years setting, it is easy to fall into the trap of offering superficial feedback or what has been called 'plastic praise'. In other words, we offer 'nice words' that really do not mean anything and certainly do not mean anything educationally. Consider the following words and phrases that can often be heard in a setting:

- wonderful

- super

- fantastic

- great

- excellent

- very good

- well done.

If we use these words, then there is a danger that a gifted and talented child who has completed the task but not really put in much effort or learned anything new will think this is an acceptable level of effort. In other words, if the educator is happy with this effort, why should the child put in more? In this way, gifted and talented children can start to learn to underachieve. Another problem with this kind of feedback is that while children are likely to know that these words are positive, they do not really give any clues as to what it is that is wonderful, super, fantastic, and so on. If the child wants to build on their success, then they require much more detailed feedback. More helpful comments would include:

- You measured that sand accurately.

- I liked the way you made sure that was glued firmly.

- I saw you try several pieces of the jigsaw before you found the one that fits.

- I noticed you listened closely to the story.

- You coloured in round the edges carefully.

These kinds of comments show the child that you have really observed what they have been doing and that you appreciate how they have tackled a task. In this way the child can:

- repeat the approach on another occasion

- clarify the learning that has taken place

- make connections between the activity and the required outcomes.

Another area to consider is the non-verbal feedback we give children. This includes all the body language we use when no word is spoken. Some children fail to read the non-verbal cues we give them as adults, but others are only too aware of them. Think of the kind of non-verbal cues we might give that encourage children:

- smile

- nod of the head

- thumbs up

- pat on the shoulder (note: children dislike being patted on the head!)

- hand clapping

- wink.

These non-verbal cues indicate that things are going well and the child should continue. However, like one-word comments, they do not tell us which aspects are going well and should be continued. Other non-verbal cues include:

- frown

- shake of the head

- rolling the eyes

- 'wagging of the finger'

- raising eyebrows

- thumbs down.

These indicate that all is not well. Again, they do not give the child a clear indication of what aspects should be stopped or how to improve.

### Cross reference

Table 7.1 on page 79 suggests words and phrases that contribute to the learner's identity – some positively, some negatively. We can see here the importance of our words in relation to learner identity.

Effective feedback needs to be related to learning. If we are to ensure it helps children to develop positive learning identities, then we have to consider carefully what we say and do. Reflecting on our choice of words or actions will help us to see where we need to develop practice.

### Cross reference

Figure 7.1 on page 79 shows how we can reflect on our feedback.

**Table 7.1    Things to say**

| Things to say | Impact | Things to avoid saying | Impact |
|---|---|---|---|
| 'I like the way you have used colour in that picture' | This allows the child to understand what it is in particular that they have done well | 'That's a good picture' | The focus is on the end product and not the process. What exactly is it that's good about it? |
| 'You really took your time with that and tried very hard to match the shapes' | This suggests that they succeeded in the task by taking their time and trying hard. While ability is important, this statement allows the child to see that other things matter too | 'You're a really clever boy/girl' | This suggests that ability is innate and nothing to do with effort. When this child meets something they cannot do, they are likely to think they are 'stupid' |
| 'Do you think it would look different if …' | There is an acceptance of the finished product and the suggestion is about enhancing it | 'That's quite good but …' | Feedback is imprecise and the 'but' suggests there is now going to be criticism |
| 'I liked how you chose coloured circles to stick on to your card. It can be hard to keep the glue in the right place but the tub should help you' | The child's work is acknowledged. The child does not feel they have done anything wrong and have been given advice on how to keep the glue in the right place. | 'That's a nice card you made but keep the glue on the paper' | Imprecise feedback as to why the card is 'nice' and the emphasis is on housekeeping |

**Figure 7.1    Reflecting on feedback**

| Date | Learning experience | One-word feedback | Learning-related phrase | Non-verbal feedback |
|---|---|---|---|---|
| 12/02/07 | Jigsaws | Good | N/A | Smile |
| 23/02/07 | Outdoor play | N/A | Have another go but this time try to walk over the logs without falling off | Thumbs up |
| 05/03/07 | Sand | Excellent | Your castle is still standing up. Why did it work this time? | Smile |
| 16/05/07 | Computer | No | N/A | Wagging finger |

Reflecting on our feedback in a variety of areas will allow us to see if we adopt particular approaches. Are there some areas where we feel more skilled to give useful feedback than others? Are there activities and areas where health and safety dictate what we say and do? If there are, do we explain why some measures are necessary or do we leave the child thinking they are in the wrong? The chart on page 80 will help you to think about your use of feedback. Take time to consider what you do and say. Better still, ask a colleague to observe you as you work with children.

## Reflecting on feedback

**Key worker** _____

| Date | Learning experience | Learning feedback | Learning-related phrase | Non-verbal feedback |
|------|---------------------|-------------------|-------------------------|---------------------|
|      |                     |                   |                         |                     |
|      |                     |                   |                         |                     |
|      |                     |                   |                         |                     |
|      |                     |                   |                         |                     |

 **Photocopiable**

Practitioners need to think about when they give feedback and how often they give it. Young children require frequent meaningful feedback while they are undertaking the activity. This gives them confidence to progress and move on with the task. If you wait too long, the child may have moved on from the task and their focus will have changed. They may also require to re-visit the feedback before starting another task. This allows the child to build on the learning that took place previously.

Feedback is crucial for several reasons:

1. It moves the learning forward.

2. It impacts on the child's beliefs about themselves as a learner.

3. It lets the child know how they are doing.

The wrong kind of feedback can leave a child feeling vulnerable and insecure. Some gifted and talented children can be highly sensitive and have strong reactions to others. If we want to impact positively on the child's learning, then we have to think about what we say and how we say it.

## Staff working together

A difficulty can arise in a setting where particular members of staff adopt a particular approach but others do not. This can be confusing for the child and, in the case of feedback, can certainly leave the child very uncertain as to their position as a learner. This morning their enquiring questions were welcomed and encouraged; this afternoon they are told they ask too many questions and they should just finish the picture. To avoid this scenario, it is necessary to consider how you will implement a constructive approach to feedback across the setting. There are some steps the setting can follow:

1. Agree a time when the staff come together to discuss learning issues within the setting. An explanation of the area under consideration should be given. It should include evidence of why this area has been selected as an area for exploration. This could be done by managers or particular members of staff, or an outside speaker could be invited to talk to the staff.

2. Staff should be given the opportunity to think about and discuss the issue. All comments should be valued and accepted. Interactive methods are likely to work best. For example, a series of statements can be displayed. These should be deliberately ambiguous or controversial – 'We should always say nice things to children'. Staff should be asked to 'vote with their feet' by going to one of three points in the room – agree, disagree, not sure/don't know. Staff have to be prepared to justify why they have selected their stance. Debate and discussion will follow relating to the use of language in the statements, meanings of words, and so on. Having heard the differing viewpoints, staff can be offered the opportunity to change their position.

3. Staff should now consider their own experiences and the impact feedback has had on them. They should highlight feedback that has encouraged them and feedback that has affected them negatively. Links now have to be made between this and their practice with children.

4. Staff can draw up an agreement for giving feedback for the setting. This agreement should guide and scaffold what staff say and do. Sometimes getting conformity at this point will be hard, but do not give up! Compromise may be necessary at first. Staff could start with agreeing how they will give feedback during outdoor play for example. Having implemented and evaluated this, they can tweak the agreement if necessary and then begin including it into other curricular areas.

A chart could be displayed on the wall, highlighting phrases staff in the setting are trying to use. This way everyone, including parents, can see the approach being adopted within the setting.

Table 7.2    In this setting we are trying to ...

| I this setting we are trying to say ... | In this setting we are trying to avoid saying ... |
| --- | --- |
| 'That's really good, tell me why you put that bit there' | 'That's really good' |
| 'You ask lots of questions, think of your three best questions and ask me those' | 'You never stop asking questions' |
| 'You're trying really hard' | 'You're very clever' |
| 'Let us try working this out together. We've all got good ideas' | 'You need to work with each other' |
| 'If we can all settle down we'll be able to hear this idea' | 'Stop talking' |

Although I am suggesting that we try to give accurate but positive feedback, we have to acknowledge that this is not always easy. How we are feeling, the experiences we have had prior to arriving at work, and our general health will affect our ability to structure comments that are supportive and accurate. It is not only children's behaviour that is affected by their feelings. We also need to acknowledge that for some staff members this will be a different way of thinking, and as such it may take time for the changes in approach to become embedded in practice. In addition, we need to try to ensure we talk to each other in ways that are supportive and encouraging. Creating a supportive workplace for ourselves is as important as creating a supportive learning environment for children.

Throughout this process it is important to bear in mind that the purpose of all this is to ensure that we are helping gifted and talented young children, and indeed all young children, to develop positive learner identities.

## Working alongside parents

If we accept that we learn better when we learn with and from each other, and if we accept that feedback is important, then this has to apply to our work with parents. Parents see their children in many different contexts and, while parents can never be completely objective about their child, we need to accept that they know their children much better than we do. It is therefore vital that we pull our knowledge together to ensure we do our best for the children in our care. If the setting has identified that a child has particular abilities, then they should meet with the parent(s) to talk this through. Some parents will have been aware from an early age that their child was able to do things earlier than expected, and may well be pleased that the setting has recognized this. Others will be completely surprised that their child has shown aptitude for activities, and will need time to come to terms with what this means. The vast majority of the parents I speak to are keen to work with staff and are realistic about their child and their abilities. They are concerned not to come across as 'pushy parents' and, like our early years settings, they want the best for their child. When I work with staff there are two recurring concerns when talking about parents. One relates to 'pushy parents' and the other to parents who want the setting to work to their schedule. Some parents send their child to a different club or organization every night while others have their child repeat endless pages of sums or have them practise writing, in the belief this will somehow make them 'gifted and talented' and give them a 'good start'. Sometimes these unrealistic expectations can cause high levels of anxiety for children. In both these situations, talking to the parents is crucial. Discussing such things as child development, the ways children learn and active learning approaches, for example, will allow the setting to explain their approach to learning and teaching. It also offers an opportunity for the setting to reassure the parent that you both have the same goal in mind – offering the best care and learning opportunity for the child. From this discussion, enriching activities can be outlined. Ways parents and the setting can work together could include:

- talking to the child as much as possible to increase their vocabulary

    - commenting on things around you as you travel in the car, bus, walk along the pavement

    - talking about their day at the setting

    - talking through options when making decisions

    - talking through everyday occurrences

- providing a range of toys that encourage logical thinking, spatial awareness, imaginative play

    - puzzles

    - chess

    - draughts

    - jigsaws

    - dressing-up clothes

    - an assortment of boxes

- answering their child's questions

  - answers should contain explanations as well as answers. For example, 'You have to wash your hands before you eat because there are lots of bacteria on them and some of the bacteria might make you feel sick'

  - answering questions with another question can help the child to think more deeply. For example, 'Yes, we could put the box there but what might happen if we do?'

- asking good questions of their child

  - during everyday activities questions can be built in that make the child think. For example, why is the sponge hard until we put it into the water? How can we fit all of these things into the big box? What do you think has happened to the ice?

- reading to and with their child

  - provide a range of different kinds of books including fiction, non-fiction, poetry

  - choose books with repetitive phrases, encourage the child to join in with these

  - talk about the shape of words

  - talk about how the story is constructed. Stories have a beginning, a middle and an end

  - talk about different characters

  - use book- and literature-related words such as cover, illustrator, author, plot, spine, index, contents page, fiction, non-fiction.

All these activities are likely to be offered by the setting. They are offering them because they are important to a child's development. This is not an 'education knows best' approach but it is about working together to offer opportunities that help shape a child as they grow and develop. If the setting is adopting the feedback approach outlined in this book, then it would do well to discuss this with parents. What parents say to children can affect them deeply. Discussing the kind of feedback the setting is using can allow parents to consider their own approach. I am not suggesting here that the setting tells parents what to say. My experience of working with parents has been that when you explain the approach adopted within the setting it causes many of them to reflect on what they say. Often they admit that out of frustration or a lack of patience at what was often the end of a long day, they have berated their child, and many admit to deeply regretting it afterwards. We need to acknowledge that as educators and as parents we will not always get it right, we are after all human, and so we will have days when it is easy to think rationally and consider each word we say and other days when it will not be easy.

While the ideas outlined above will support staff as they seek to work alongside parents, we also have to accept that there will be some parents who will not agree with the approach I am suggesting. When this happens, we have to accept this position and support the child within the setting to ensure that whatever approach is adopted within the family, the setting is consistent in its feedback and approach to the child.

When I asked parents what they would have liked early years settings to have done to support their gifted and talented child, they told me that they wished the setting had believed them when they told them their child was gifted and talented. Given that parents are the most accurate predictors of children who are gifted and talented, settings would do well to listen to and believe parents. Settings and parents need to gather evidence about the child, analyse that evidence and plan and work together to ensure that the child is being challenged. We should never lose sight of the fact that all the adults involved have the same goal – the best for the child. The differences occur in the way we reach that goal. Working together, rather than creating a 'them and us' mentality, will help us to reach that common goal more amicably. A child who leaves the setting as a confident individual with a positive learner identity will bring satisfaction to both parents and staff.

## Sending messages

All our words, actions, looks and body language send intentional and sometimes unintentional messages to those around us. Gifted and talented children are often more 'in tune' with some of the nuances of body language, 'sighs', eye rolling, and so on, and therefore we have to think carefully about the messages we are conveying to them. Consider therefore the following case studies.

 **Case studies**

### Ronald

Ronald loved the setting and was good at everything. He had started to read, he had a good singing voice, he enjoyed the challenging puzzles he was being given, he was popular with the other children in the setting, and his art and design work was excellent and had won a prize in a national competition. His dad approached the setting to say that recently Ronald had been complaining of a sore tummy in the morning, saying he did not want to go to nursery, and he was very worried about him. Following some careful investigation, it was discovered that Ronald was finding the setting stressful. He liked all the activities but always being told how good he was made him feel he had to get everything right otherwise he would be letting people down. Although in the setting he seemed to be doing well and was still confident and outgoing, his anxieties had become apparent at home.

*(Continued)*

*(Continued)*

Feeling that you have to be perfect all the time can lead gifted and talented children to underachieve so that expectations lower. In an effort to offer challenge, we sometimes overload gifted and talented children with extra tasks and responsibilities followed by huge amounts of praise when they succeed at them. If they are anxious to please you, as young children often are, they will not want to, or know how to, say no and will not want to let you down. We need to think carefully about what we ask children to do.

### Amie

Amie and four friends were working with their key worker. They were discussing 'people who help us'. They were talking about the fire services. Amie clearly knew a lot about firemen/women, fire engines and emergencies. Amie was also keen that her key worker would know how much she knew. Part of the way into the discussion, Amie began to realize that it was not what the key worker wanted to hear because she hardly ever asked Amie any questions. Indeed the key worker said 'You seem to know all about the fire services, let someone else have a chance to answer questions'. Amie spent the rest of the session listening to things she already knew. She also learnt that it is not always good to know things other people do not.

In this kind of situation we need to consider how we can utilize the knowledge a child has. It may be that we need to have a one-to-one session with them at another time. While we would not consciously tell a child 'You know too much, be quiet', unconsciously this may be the message the child receives.

### Meryl

Meryl was the kind of child who was 'into everything'. She flitted from one activity to another and rarely settled to complete anything. She loved painting but often got as much paint on herself as she did on the paper. She was described as a tomboy and loved outdoor play, often challenging the boys to climb higher, run faster, shout louder, and so on. She excelled at construction activities often spending time creating elaborate feats of engineering. Staff in the setting had a 'soft spot' for her, turning a blind eye to much of what she got up to. They would often just roll their eyes and say 'Typical Meryl, she's such a tomboy, she's just like her brothers'.

Avoiding comparison is important when giving feedback. No two children are the same. Being compared with her brothers will not necessarily help Meryl and neither will it help them. By turning a blind eye to certain behaviour, we may be sending mixed messages not only to Meryl, but to the other children. By adopting the attitude of 'That's just Meryl', we may miss opportunities to challenge her abilities as we may not think she is capable of more.

As educators, we need to be monitoring constantly what we do and what we say. Talking to children will help us to understand how they are interpreting events in the setting – the messages we think we are sending may not be the messages they are receiving. Knowing our children well will make giving feedback a much easier process. We will know what certain individuals respond to and we can tailor our feedback accordingly. This applies not only to the children we work with, but to the adults as well. At the heart of effective feedback lies effective relationships.

### Summary

Some key points and suggestions have been made in this chapter in relation to feedback for gifted and talented young learners.

As educators we need to be aware of the dangers of the following:

- the disempowering language we use
- the negative non-verbal cues we give
- one-word feedback that tells the learner nothing.

As educators we need to:

- give verbal feedback that is linked to learning dispositions and outcomes
- be explicit about what is good/needs development
- give feedback during and after activities
- acknowledge it may take time to embed this approach fully in our practice
- work together with parents
- work together as a team
- know our children well if we are to provide constructive feedback.

### To think about

- Think about the language you use to motivate children.
- Do I give feedback that relates to learning?
- Do the children know what I expect from them?
- Are parents an integral part of the setting?
- Do I believe parents or am I suspicious of what they say?
- Do I know the children well enough so I can tailor appropriate feedback for them?

### Further reading 📖

Clarke, S. (2003) *Enriching Feedback in the Primary Classroom*. London: Hodder Murray.

Hart, B. and Risley, T.R. (1995) *Meaningful Differences in Everyday Parenting and Intellectual Development in Young American Children*. Baltimore MD: Paul H. Brookes.

Hart, B. and Risley, T.R. (1999) *The Social World of Children Learning to Talk*. Baltimore, MD: Paul H. Brookes.

# 8

# All-round development of gifted young learners

Some key points about the general development of young learners are made in this chapter.

> • **Working with gifted and talented young learners is a privilege and a challenge.**
> • **We can contribute positively or negatively to a child's all-round development.**
> • **Gifted and talented children may display overexcitabilities.**
> • **We need to nurture and develop learning dispositions and attitudes.**
> • **We face challenges as we seek to plan for learning.**
> • **We need to accept children for who they are and what they can do.**

Working with any young child will be a mixture of fun, pleasure and challenge. There will be days when it is hard and we feel like finding another job. There will be other days when the learning falls into place and we are rewarded with a grin, laughter and a sparkle in a child's eye that comes from the sheer joy of learning. Working with young children is an enormous privilege and one that we should not take lightly.

We are involved with children as they develop emotionally, socially, physically, intellectually and linguistically. While we are not the only influence on each of these areas, we can nonetheless contribute positively and/or negatively to their development.

Gifted and talented children can sometimes seem to possess extraordinary amounts of excess energy. This extra energy results in an urge to explore the world. These surges in energy can come from boredom or from the excitement of new ideas. A Polish psychologist, Kazimierz Dabrowski (1964; 1972), describes these 'overexcitabilities'. Dabrowski suggests there are five overexcitabilities:

1. Emotional.

2. Intellectual.

3. Imaginational.

4. Psychomotor.

5. Sensual.

There seems to be a higher number of gifted and talented children, especially when compared with their age peers, who display these traits. This means that gifted and talented children can be sensitive in a number of areas resulting in a stronger reactions to things, which are sustained for a longer time than might be expected.

## 1   Emotional overexcitability

Children with emotional overexcitability might have, for example, intense feelings of concern. This concern might be for others who make up their circle of friends and family, and as a result they have an ability to empathize. We might say they have strong inter-personal and intra-personal skills. Their concern might also be for world events, animal welfare or the environment. Children in your setting may well have seen disturbing news reports of famine, drought, earthquakes or other natural disasters. They may have intense feelings about these incidents but may also be aware that they have no control over them. As such, this disturbs them greatly. They may also feel a sense of intense loneliness.

## 2   Intellectual overexcitability

A child might be constantly asking searching questions. They want to know lots of things about a particular topic that has caught their interest, and once they have this knowledge they will want to analyse it. They have an intense curiosity and want to work out problems; in fact they go looking for problems. They might be extremely observant and often connect new knowledge with existing knowledge in order to come to a new understanding. A child like this in the setting can become challenging – intellectually, physically and emotionally – while catering appropriately for all.

## 3   Imaginational overexcitability

Children here are inventive and delight in images and visualization. Linguistically they are interested in metaphors and images. They are interested in poetic opportunities and drama. They might engage in inventive role play or want to tell you things through images. They may also daydream or have imaginary friends.

## 4   Psychomotor overexcitability

This results in a child appearing to have a surplus of energy. They will constantly move and engage in physical activity, talk rapidly and seek out action. The child will derive great pleasure from engaging in this, but it can be relentless and tiring for those they live with as well as for their friends and educators. In the setting, these children will be constantly moving around and wriggling about. They will lie across the table, twirl their hair, tap their feet or drum their fingers. In short, they will engage in behaviours that we often try to stop as they can be distracting and annoying to others.

## 5    Sensual overexcitability

Sensual overexcitability is linked to the senses. They will gain great pleasure from art, music and language, and will be intrigued by textures, smells, taste, sounds and sights. Great aesthetic pleasure will be gained from things such as scenes of nature or a particular piece of music. Some children will find labels on clothes annoying, they may also find bright lights distracting. They will possibly like to be the centre of attention. In the setting, this might mean they always volunteer for 'star roles' or find ways to be in the limelight.

Dabrowski suggests that the strength of these five overexcitabilities in conjunction with ability will allow us to see a child's developmental promise. If this is true, then we need to consider how we can influence a young child's beliefs about themselves as a learner. We have to think about what we say and do when working alongside the children in our care. Planning appropriate learning experiences means that we have to consider a child's intellectual ability as well as their social and emotional development. We have to ensure that we contribute positively to their learner identities.

## The pros and cons of supporting gifted and talented children

Torrance (1981) worked with gifted and talented creative children. When they had grown up, they were asked to think about teachers who had made a difference to them. Some common themes emerged in their answers. Let us see what they said made a difference and what this might mean in an early years setting. People who made a difference to gifted and talented children did the following things.

### Let the child know that their ideas, emotions and behaviours were important

The way adults act and react to children and their ideas, comments and chatter is of crucial importance. We need not always engage in deep discussions with a child (although we might), but we do have to acknowledge positively that the child has said something. Some gifted and talented young children enjoy talking to adults since adults understand what they are saying in a way that their peers do not. Simply smiling, asking a question about what has been said, saying that their comment is really interesting but that you do not have time to talk about it just now, can let the child know that you have valued what they had to say. Gifted and talented young children can sometimes behave in ways that are older than their years. As adults, we should not be surprised at this, neither should we be surprised when they behave in an age-appropriate way. We need to help young gifted and talented children understand the discrepancy between their advanced ability and their age behaviours and emotions.

## Valued the child's unique ability

Early years professionals are well used to observing children and using those observations to plan activities. During this process we will begin to see each child's profile develop. All the children in our care will demonstrate abilities. We should be valuing the abilities of all children, regardless of the level of these abilities. While gifted and talented young children may work alone from time to time, we must ensure that the children know that their abilities are welcomed in our setting and that they contribute to the rich tapestry that make up our early years community.

## Spent quality time with the child

In a busy setting it can be easy to overlook particular individuals. A young gifted child may happily engage in challenging activities in isolation but they will also relish the opportunity to speak to an adult in depth about things they are passionately interested in. As we prepare our weekly plans, we need to ensure that at some point we build in time to talk and work with gifted and talented young children. That time should be theirs and we should not be distracted by other activities and children. It need not always be the same person, it need not happen every day and it does not have to be a great amount of time. Fifteen minutes of quality interaction can be of great value and leave the child feeling that their abilities and, more importantly, they as a person are appreciated.

## Offered support for trying, not just for getting it right

Some gifted and talented children can have perfectionist tendencies. This can cause difficulties as they constantly try to complete every activity 'perfectly' or they strive to get everything 'right'. We need to ensure in our feedback that we encourage mistakes, that we help children to learn from those mistakes and that we offer activities where there may be more than one right answer. We need to allow children to see us as adults make mistakes and to see us work through things in a trial and error approach.

## Valued the whole child and not just their particular abilities

Some gifted and talented children will be good at one particular area, for example, reading; others will show ability in every curricular area. On the one hand, a danger can arise if the setting simply pushes the child on in the area they have shown ability. On the other, a danger can arise if we simply work on the areas where there are concerns and difficulties. We need to take into consideration the whole child. We need to challenge particular abilities as they develop but at the same time ensure we are offering rounded opportunities to young children.

## Allowed the child to explore their feelings

All young children need support as they make sense of the feelings and emotions they are experiencing. The connection between behaviour and feelings is not one that children readily make. Talking with the child and helping them to make that connection can be vital to their development; such as 'I think you knew which jigsaw piece fitted there and it made you grumpy when Gavin tried to put it in the wrong place. Because you were feeling grumpy, you pushed the jigsaws off the table'. The use of pictures can also be helpful and allow children to explore body language. When we have a better understanding of our feelings and emotions – positive and negative – then we can better control them, change them or repeat them.

## Supported the child as they followed their particular interests

When the setting has identified that children have a particular interest in a subject, topic or curricular area, they can seek to develop that interest. Within the setting, books and the Internet can be used to provide further information. The setting can explore if there are any clubs or organizations that meet and which the child could attend outside the setting. 'Experts' can be invited to speak with the individual, a group or the whole setting. Again it is vital that the setting does not dismiss the interest as a fad, bizarre or unimportant but that we search for ways of developing that interest alongside the regular features of an early years curriculum.

## Worked with the child, modelling cooperation

Bruner (1996) suggests that we learn through collaboration. Learning alongside others is important for all children. When the child has the opportunity to work alongside a more knowledgeable other and engage in observational learning, they learn from and with that individual. If there are certain learning behaviours we want children to develop such as investigative skills, thinking skills and problem-solving skills, then we need to model these for the children in our care. Some gifted and talented children will connect more readily with adults in the setting as their cognitive abilities are ahead of their age peers. It is important to offer opportunities for them to work with intellectual peers as well as their age peers. Staff in the setting, experts from outside, older pupils can all be good role models for young children.

Supporting young children in these ways will allow them to thrive. Not only will gifted and talented children soar but those who find learning difficult will also benefit. The themes above are not unique or special to gifted and talented pupils. These are things effective practitioners do for all children.

Learning should be an exciting activity for us all. Young children should leave our settings secure in the learning dispositions that will enable them to continue their learning journey. These dispositions will include:

- *Enthusiasm* – if a child is enthusiastic about something then they will approach tasks with a confident attitude. They can enthuse – enthusiasm can be infectious! Their enthusiasm can carry over into other activities.

- *Perseverance* – some children establish a pattern early on of 'giving up' if tasks are hard or another topic takes their interest. Working through a task to some kind of conclusion is important.

- *Respect for others* – to live in our global society it is crucial that children can work alongside others. While they do not have to be 'best friends' with everyone, they need to coexist.

- *Experimentation* – we need to make sure children are not afraid to experiment with ideas and concepts. Trying things out, reaching conclusions, endeavouring to do things in new and creative ways will all contribute to a child's knowledge and understanding of the world around them.

- *Cooperation* – learning through working together towards a common goal or purpose will allow children to negotiate, support, challenge and have greater understanding of what it means to work with each other.

- *Acceptance* – settings, which understand and accept that we all have different abilities, and which view this diversity as a strength, will help children to grow up with a healthy acceptance for those who are in some way 'different' from themselves.

- *Curiosity* – in the UK the old saying goes 'curiosity killed the cat'. However, curiosity or inquisitiveness is crucial if we are to help children to develop enquiring and inspiring minds. Asking good questions and finding out how things work and why will help to develop understanding and knowledge.

- *Concentration* – we need to encourage children to engage with tasks and not to 'flit' from one to another where, at best, surface learning will take place. We need to build up concentration through short, interesting and engaging activities.

- *Confidence* – to take on new and challenging tasks and to risk-take requires a certain amount of confidence. As children build up a positive learner identity they will increase in confidence so that they see challenge as something to be grasped with both hands and not avoided at all costs.

- *Self-motivation* – while as early years practitioners we cannot motivate children, we can create the right environment that allows children to become motivated. This is achieved by allowing children to have a say in their learning, making sure goals are achievable, valuing learners, having high expectations for them and ensuring any praise we use is 'real' and meaningful.

Much of the above, and what this book has talked about generally, relates to the idea of beliefs about ourselves as learners or self-efficacy. Indeed, it could be argued that it is this idea that underpins all learning and attitudes to learning. Self-efficacy is the belief that you can approach unknown activities and events (Bandura, 1986). Where self-efficacy is high then confidence and self-esteem will be too. Self-efficacy affects

- the choices we make

- the effort we expend on a task

- how long we will persist when the task is difficult

- how we feel about the task.

Where we have regulated children's learning, left little opportunity for choice and given negative feedback for example, self-efficacy may be low. Where children have contributed to their learning, made choices about their learning and have developed a positive belief in themselves as a learner then self-efficacy is likely to be high. Thus high self-efficacy will result in children making positive choices, putting in a great deal of effort, persisting even in the face of difficulty and having positive feelings about themselves as a learner.

The very nature of early years education offers wonderful opportunities to nurture and develop these beliefs, dispositions and attitudes. Where children feel valued, secure, safe and respected, then they are more likely to take risks, work together and solve problems. Many of the ideas discussed above will seem to be obvious. Why then do we find them so hard to do?

## Time

There never seems to be enough time in the day for all that needs to be done. Other events and incidental interruptions mean that well-planned activities do not happen. Often these are unforeseen, small and insignificant operational duties that have a major impact on learning and teaching. Initiatives such as tooth brushing or a session of daily physical activity mean that we have to find the time to allow these things to happen. Staff are also involved in clearing up accidents, coordinating visits and taking their group to the gym at their allotted time. As a result, quality observation time can easily disappear.

## Range of needs

Children come to the setting with all kinds of needs that have to be met. These may be physical, emotional, behavioural, linguistic, academic or social and can seem daunting and frustrating for staff as they plan meaningful learning experiences for all.

## Staff absence

Staff absence can mean higher staff: child ratio. It may also result in a succession of supply staff who have to be briefed on activities and routines.

## Conflicting demands

There are a number of conflicting demands on staff time. Rightly, there is an expectation that outdoor play will take place, however, the dressing of children for outdoor play in winter takes up a disproportionate amount of time. An open-door policy for working with parents is important, but being available to speak to parents as needs arise can disrupt the flow of the session.

What can we do to make things easier? There are no magic solutions to the issues outlined above. However, there are things we can do that will refocus us:

- *Remember why we're there*. It can become all too easy to get caught up in routines, structures and systems. We can lose sight of why we are there. Early years should be about fostering a love of learning through play.

- *Keep the child at the centre*. When systems, structures and routines dominate then we will be in danger of losing sight of the child. Where learning experiences keep the child at the centre then we will be more likely to spend time concentrating on learning and teaching.

- *Try out new ideas*. To avoid complacency it is vital that we take risks and try out new ideas. Just as children learn from challenging experiences, we will also.

- *Keep a sense of humour*. While learning is a serious business, we need to maintain a sense of humour. Gifted and talented children will often see and appreciate the inconsistencies in situations; perhaps we should too.

## Confident children with a love of learning

Developing the child's learner identity is crucial if they are to leave us believing they can learn. Gifted and talented young children need to feel their abilities are valued and accepted. The following (true) extract demonstrates that the wrong word from us can have a lasting impact: 'Went to College, then went to University and got a first class degree. See Mrs X, I could succeed in something (she was my first teacher, and well let's just say she didn't think much of me)'.

Each child in our care is unique. In the case of gifted and talented children it may be that some of the things that make them unique is their ability to:

- concentrate for long periods of time

- have and use large vocabularies for their age

- be interested in a range of topics

- understand the subtleties of language

- read and/or write

- ask endless questions

- see alternatives

- present original, sometimes quirky, ideas

- use reason and logic when suggesting answers

- see the big picture.

We need to accept these children for who they are and what they can do. We need to help them to create a learner identity that results in an endless love of learning, that preserves their natural curiosity, that increases their motivation to learn and to explore their worlds, and that captures that initial excitement about learning.

I had been working with some children on dance, music and drama activities, and at the same time a colleague had been working with staff considering how best to support gifted and talented children. When the staff joined the children at the end of the day, they were intrigued to know what their 'teachers' had been doing. My colleague told them that they had been working hard too, and had been learning about things they could do in their setting that would make learning more exciting and challenging. One little boy raised his hand and said 'Oh they've been doing lifelong learning'. Let us hope that all children leave our settings feeling confident and secure to continue on the journey of lifelong learning.

 Summary

Some key points and suggestions have been made in this chapter and in this book in relation to the all-round development of gifted and talented young learners.

- Be aware of our own learner identity.

- Know that learning identities change depending on context.

- Actions are based on theories or beliefs, we need to know what we believe – and be willing to change.

- We need to have shared narratives and understandings so we can support gifted and talented young children.

- We need to plan challenging activities.

- Children and practitioners are partners in the learning experience.

- Providing challenging activities will allow us to identify gifted and talented young children.

- Observation is key to providing appropriate learning experiences.

- We should avoid plastic praise.

- Feedback should be linked to learning.

- We need to nurture and develop learning dispositions and attitudes.

- We need to accept children for who they are and what they can do.

**To think about**

- Have I thought about the many abilities young children bring to the setting?
- How does the setting actively celebrate and develop these abilities?
- In what ways do I contribute positively to children's learner identity?
- Do children leave the setting with a love of learning?

# Appendix

If you go to the SAGE website and search for the entry for this book www.sagepub.co.uk/sutherland, you will be able to download PDFs of the material included in this Appendix and of the photocopiable material included in the body of the book.

## FACTSHEETS FOR STAFF

The following information is for practitioners. This information is intended as a starting point. You will be able to find out much more in-depth information from books and websites, however, the outline below can be used as the basis for discussion and for further topics for exploration by children and yourself!

# FACTSHEET

## STARS

- The Earth is surrounded by stars. When there are no clouds in our night sky, we can see the stars clearly.

- The Sun is actually a star. The reason it looks so different is because it is so close to us.

- We can see patterns in the stars. Different civilizations saw different patterns and they thought they related to their gods.

- In the southern hemisphere (Antarctica, parts of Africa and Asia, Australia, most of Southern America), you will find the following constellations:

  - Aquarius (the Water-Bearer)
  - Orion (the Hunter)
  - Scorpio (the Scorpion)
  - Southern Cross
  - Hydra (Water Snake)
  - Libra (Scales)

- In the northern hemisphere (Europe, 2/3 of Africa north of the Congo River, North America, Central America, small part of South America north of the Amazon River, Asia, although Indonesia is primarily in the southern hemisphere), you will find the following constellations:

  - Pegasus
  - Perseus
  - Pole star
  - Plough (or Little Bear)
  - Great Bear
  - Leo (the Lion)

- Stars look small but they are in fact huge balls of hot gas. They look small because they are so far away.

- Stars would be just like our Sun if you were close to them.

- Galaxies are made up of billions of stars. On a clear night we can see part of our galaxy. It is known as the Milky Way.

- There are billions of galaxies in space, each made up of billions of individual stars.

- Galaxies are grouped into clusters, groups of clusters are known as super clusters.

- All the galaxies, clusters of galaxies and super clusters together make up our universe.

- A shooting star is really smaller pieces of dust from space. They are known as meteoroids. Some of these are quite small, as small as a grain of sand, but others are quite big. They are travelling so fast that as they pass through the Earth's atmosphere they burn up as they fall to Earth, but some are too big to burn and cause damage when they land on Earth. A hundred years ago a meteor landed in Siberia and exploded like an atomic bomb.

- When a star comes to the end of its life, it can explode. Supernovae are the biggest explosions in the universe.

- Once a star has exploded as a supernova, the bit that is left shrinks quickly. If it is big, it shrinks to almost nothing. The area of space that is left has enormous gravity. This gravity sucks in any other nearby material, including other stars. This is known as a black hole.

- Black holes are called black holes because gravity is so strong not even light can escape from it.

- Stars come in different colours. The colour is related to the temperature of the star. Hot stars are blue. Cooler stars are red. Hot stars can be 30,000°C. Cooler stars are as little as 1000°C.

- The temperature of a star is related to its mass.

- The solar system includes the following:

  - the Sun
  - the inner planets – Mercury, Venus, Earth, Mars
  - the outer planets – Jupiter, Saturn, Uranus, Neptune
  - the dwarf planets – Pluto, Eris, Ceres
  - small solar system bodies – asteroids, comets, meteors and meterorites, near Earth objects

 **Photocopiable**

# FACTSHEET

**THE SUN**

- The Sun is the one star we can see in great detail.

- The Sun is not solid but made up of gases – hydrogen, helium and small amounts of 90 other elements.

- Number facts:

  - The Sun is 149.6 million kilometres away from Earth. This is close in space terms!
  - The diameter (width) of the Sun is approximately 1.4 million kilometres (about 109 times that of the Earth).
  - The surface we can see is 5,500°C.
  - The core is 15 million°C.

- The Sun looks like it is burning but it is actually exploding.

- The Sun fires out invisible particles into space. When these pass the North and South Poles they can make the air glow.

- The Sun is a relatively cool star. Its temperature is about 6000°C.

- We just see the outside surface of the Sun, inside the sun there are unimaginably violent explosions going on. Some children will be ready to use the correct terminology for the process:

  - Inside our Sun atoms of hydrogen gas fuse (or join together) to form another gas called helium. This is known as nuclear fusion and is where the Sun's energy comes from.
  - This energy travels outwards to the surface of the Sun, throwing hot gases millions of miles into space before the Sun's gravity pulls it back.
  - Heat, light and radiation stream off the Sun into space.

# FACTSHEET

## SPACE EXPLORATION

- All early civilizations studied the night sky, for example the Babylonians, the Egyptians, the ancient Chinese, the Mayan people of South America. Even Stonehenge was probably for studying the sky.

- Hans Lippershey from the Netherlands, built the first telescope in 1608.

- Galileo, from Italy, was one of the first people to use a telescope to study the night sky. He first recorded his observations in 1609–1610.

- Edwin Hubble, an American, was the first person to show us that there are other galaxies. The Hubble telescope is named after him.

- Robert Oppenheimer is another famous astronomer. He helped us to understand more about black holes and neutron stars.

- Telescopes collect light and other kinds of energy from objects in space, record it and then use it to make images which help us find out more about the stars and planets. Some telescopes are put in space and others are put on Earth.

- Earth telescopes have been used for 400 years; space telescopes have been used in the last 40 years.

- Space probes are designed to investigate particular planets or targets. Some fly past their target, others orbit their targets and some land on their targets. We have landed space probes on the Moon, Mars, Venus and the asteroid Eros.

- We have been sending rockets into space since 1957.

- The first people went into space in 1961.

- Edwin Aldrin and Neil Armstrong were the first astronauts to land on the Moon on 20 July 1969. They were from the crew of Apollo 11.

- The International Space Station (ISS) is 230 miles/370 km above Earth. It is being built and used by 16 countries. Crews have lived on the ISS since 2000. They conduct experiments and see how things behave in space.

**Photocopiable**

'Developing the Gifted and Talented Young Learner' © Margaret Sutherland, 2008.

# GLOSSARY

**Asteroid**   A rock in space that is orbiting the sun. Most are found in the Asteroid or Main Belt.

**Astronaut**   Someone who travels into space.

**Astronomer**   Someone who studies the universe and everything in it.

**Astronomy**   The study of space.

**Astrophotographer**   Someone who takes photographs of the night sky and objects in it.

**Astrophysics**   The physics of the universe.

**Atmosphere**   Gases round a moon or planet and held in place by gravity.

**Atom**   The basic building blocks of everything in the universe.

**Billion**   One thousand million.

**Black hole**   A collapsed star that has so much gravity that everything close to it, even light, is pulled in.

**Cluster**   Stars or a group of galaxies.

**Comet**   A small object made of dust and ice. Sometimes known as a 'dirty snowball'.

**Constellation**   An area of sky where bright stars seem to form together in the shape of an animal or human.

**Crater**   A hollow on the surface of a planet, moon or asteroid formed by an asteroid colliding into it.

**Element**   Hydrogen, oxygen and carbon. A substance made up of one kind of atom.

**Equator**   An imaginary line drawn round the middle of a planet, moon or star. It divides it into the northern and southern hemispheres.

**Fireball**   A very bright meteor.

**Galaxy**   A large collection of stars, gas and dust held together by gravity.

**Gravity**   A force of attraction.

**Light year**   A unit used to measure distances across the universe. The distance light travels in one year.

**Magnetic field**   Space round a star or planet where the magnetism of the star or planet is felt.

**Mass**   The amount of material in an object. The more mass the heavier an object is.

**Meteor**   The streak of light produced by a meteor as it travels through the Earth's atmosphere.

**Meteorite**   A space rock that crashes into Earth, the Moon or another planet.

**Meteoroid**   A very small piece of dust from a comet or asteroid.

**Milky Way**   The part of our galaxy we can see at night.

**Moon**   A small planet that orbits another planet rather than the sun.

**Nebula**   A cloud of dust and gas in space.

**Nuclear reaction**   The process when elements change to other elements inside a star.

**Observatory**   The name for buildings that house telescopes.

**Orbit**   The path taken by one object round another larger object.

**Planet**   A large, round object made of rock and/or gas that orbits round a star.

**Protostar**   A star in the process of forming.

**Satellite**   An object held in orbit round a planet or moon. Human-made satellites orbit Earth. The Moon is the Earth's largest satellite.

**Solar system**   The Sun and all the objects that orbit it.

**Star**   Like our own sun, a huge flaming sphere of gases.

**Sunspot**   A cooler spot on the surface of the Sun.

**Supercluster**   Cluster of galaxies at the end of its life.

**Supernova**   An immense star that explodes and shines brightly for a few days.

**Telescope**   A piece of equipment that through the use of lens and/or mirrors collects light from a distant object and forms that light into an image.

**Trillion**   One million million (1,000,000,000,000).

**Universe**   Everything that exists.

 **Photocopiable**

# Useful websites

www.esa.int/esaKIDSen   Contains numerous pages of space-related information including our universe, lift off and life in space.

http://amazing-space.stsci.edu   A range of online activities for educators and developers.

www.darkskyscotland.org.uk   A national programme of astronomy events offering workshops, demonstrations and shows.

www.enchantedlearning.com/subjects/astronomy   A range of space-related topics giving information and activities. The section about the Sun is particularly good.

www.schoolsobservatory.org.uk   National Schools Observatory. A superb website that has activities for children aged 7–14+. The website covers Telescopes, Go observing, Universe now, Astronomy, @stroclub, International. While it is for older children, some gifted and talented children will be interested in the topics covered. There is also a section for staff called Staffroom.

http://hubblesite.org/gallery   Amazing pictures from the Hubble space telescope – a must for all your children.

www.nrao.edu/imagegallery   The site of the National Radio Astronomy Observatory. It has a photogallery of telescope and space pictures.

www.nasa.gov/audience/forkids   The US government space site offers a huge range of activities for young people.

www.lunaroutpost.com   The section 'Space Shuttle facts' is particularly good.

www.canadianspace.ca/activities   While there is some reading required for parts of this site it is a great site with the following sections:

1. Space station.
2. Astronaut school – children can see if they have quick enough reaction times when destroying asteroids, good enough hand–eye coordination and memory to be an astronaut.
3. Lift off – there is a particularly good activity about rocket trajectory.
4. Living in space – deals with issues such as food and toilets.
5. Space science.

www.discovery.com/stories/science/iss/enterstation.html   Virtual tour of the International Space Station.

www.thetech.org/exhibits/online/satellite   Build a satellite.

www.pbs.org/wgbh/nova/tothemoon    There are 360-degree panorama taken from the Apollo Moon landings. There are also audio clips of astronauts and engineers and a puzzlers section offering puzzles of varying complexity.

http://stargazers.gsfc.nasa.gov/pdf/products/books/Sun_booklet-English.htm    You can watch a movie about the Sun on this site.

www.brsc.gov.uk    The British National Space Centre. There is a 'Kids Section' with a range of activities at various levels.

www.nhm.ac.uk/nature-online/virtual-wonders/vrmeteorite.html    The Natural History Museum. You can examine meteorite exhibits.

http://planetquest.jpl.nasa.gov/gallery    Planet Quest is a site devoted to the search for another Earth. There are games, movies and simulations.

http://ology.amnh.org/astronomy    This is the American Museum of Natural History's website for children. There are many interesting areas. Astronomy is the most relevant for this topic but it also includes archaeology, Einstein, genetics, marine biology, palaeontology, Earth, mythic creatures and biodiversity.

www.seasky.org    Join the Starship Sagen on a voyage through the universe.

http://starchild.gsfc.nasa.gov    A learning centre for young astronomers.

# Supporting Gifted & Talented Pupils in the Secondary School

## Moira Thomson, Freelance Consultant, Edinburgh

'This is an excellent book which is organised for teachers, heads of schools, and those specifically involved with very able youngsters. Many ideas are provided in this book for teachers to follow in order to render their professional expertise appropriate for helping youngsters with high ability' – **Dr L.F. Lowenstein, Educational, Clinical and Forensic Psychological Consultant**

Using ideas that have been tried and tested in the classroom, this book takes a whole school approach to providing appropriate challenge and support for gifted and talented pupils in an inclusive educational setting.

**Contents**
SECTION I: IDENTIFICATION AND PROVISION / Defining giftedness / Identification of giftedness / Underachievement / Dual exceptionality / Policy and Provision / Teaching & Learning / SECTION II: SPECIFIC STRATEGIES / Differentiation / Enrichment / Acceleration / Specialist provision / Professional development

**July 2006 • 136 pages**
**Paperback (978-1-4129-1968-5) £18.99**
**Hardcover: (978-1-4129-1967-8) £63.00**

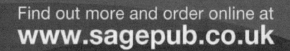

# English for Gifted and Talented Students

## 11-18 Years

## Geoff Dean, School Improvement Advisor, Milton Keynes

'This is a sourcebook of ideas and gives valuable information about the latest research on learning and teaching, as well as signposting the way forward in providing for the most able in English. It recognises the questions posed by new technologies, and gives guidance on how to harness these changes to help equip talented young people for life in the twenty first century' – *Jude Brigley, Director of Learning and Teaching at Cardiff High School, and Chair of NACE CYMRU*

Are you stuck for ways to stretch your best English students?

By focusing on what excites and motivates all learners, this book provides you with a clear guide to ensuring sound provision for your gifted and talented students.

### Contents
Why it is so important to address the needs of More Able Students in English? / Who Are the More Able in English? / Providing the Best Supportive Learning Environment for the Most Effective Development of More Able Students in English/ Learning in English/ Personalisation and Other Support Structures in English/ Activities to support and challenge More Able English Students in Secondary Schools

**April 2008 • 128 pages**
**Paperback (978-1-4129-3605-7) £19.99**
**Hardcover: (978-1-4129-3604-0) £60.00**